THE WAY OF TRANSFORMATION

*Saint Teresa of Avila on the Foundation
and Fruit of Prayer*

THE WAY OF TRANSFORMATION

Saint Teresa of Avila on the Foundation and Fruit of Prayer

MARK O'KEEFE, O.S.B.

ICS Publications
Institute of Carmelite Studies
Washington, D.C.

ICS Publications
2131 Lincoln Road NE
Washington, DC 20002-1199
800-832-8489
www.icspublications.org

© Saint Meinrad Archabbey, 2016

Published with Ecclesiastical Approval

All Scripture passages are taken from the *New Revised Standard Version: Catholic Edition, Anglicized Text*, © 1999, 1995, 1989, Division of Christian Education of the National Council of Churches of Christ in the United States of America. Used with permission.

Book and cover design and pagination by Rose Design

Cover illustration "The Way of Perfection" icon by the hand of Sister Mary Grace Melcher, O.C.D. © 2015 Terre Haute Carmel. All rights reserved. Published with permission. This icon is available on the monastery website: www.heartsawake.org

Produced and printed in the United States of America

Library of Congress Cataloging-in-Publication Data

Names: O'Keefe, Mark, 1956-author.
Title: The way of transformation : Saint Teresa of Avila on the foundation and fruit of prayer / Mark O'Keefe, O.S.B.
Description: Washington, D.C. : ICS Publications, Institute of Carmelite Studies, [2016] | Includes index.
Identifiers: LCCN 2016012773 | ISBN 9781939272393 (alk. paper)
Subjects: LCSH: Teresa, of Avila, Saint, 1515-1582. Camino de perfeccion. | Perfection—Religious aspects—Catholic Church. | God (Christianity)—Worship and love. | Prayer—Catholic Church.
Classification: LCC BX2179.T4 C3854 2016 | DDC 248.3/2—dc23
LC record available at http://lccn.loc.gov/2016012773

Contents

A Word of Thanks

The completion of my research for this book was made possible by a generous grant from the Rev. Adrian Fuerst Faculty Development Endowment of Saint Meinrad Seminary and School of Theology. I want to thank my faculty colleagues for their support of my work. I have taught an elective course at Saint Meinrad on Teresa of Avila, and I have benefited immensely from the students' interest and insights as we have read and discussed her works together.

My religious superior, Archabbot Justin DuVall, O.S.B., has generously permitted me to pursue my passion for Teresa and for John of the Cross (and my love of Spain) with my research trips to Avila over the last few summers. My former superior, Archabbot Lambert Reilly, O.S.B., kindly read an earlier form of this book and offered helpful comments and corrections. He is well known among the Carmelite communities of women in the United States, and we share a great love for St. Teresa.

I owe a debt of gratitude to Patricia Morrison and Father Marc Foley, O.C.D., of ICS Publications for their assistance and guidance through the preparation of this project. The Institute of Carmelite Studies provides an immeasurable service to the church and to those who wish to grow in prayer by their commitment to promote the study and promulgation in English of the writings of St. Teresa, St. John of the Cross, and other Carmelite authors.

I am truly blessed to serve as chaplain to the nuns of the Carmel of St. Joseph in Terre Haute, Indiana. They are a constant witness to me of the ideals of St. Teresa lived in the contemporary world. Several of the sisters read a draft of this book and offered helpful comments. I am grateful to all of the nuns for their support, prayers, and example. I dedicate this book to them.

Foreword

Torue to its title, *The Way of Transformation: Saint Teresa of Avila on the Foundation and Fruit of Prayer*, this book provides a clear and comprehensive account of the foundation and fruit of prayer as taught by St. Teresa of Avila. The author, Mark O'Keefe, O.S.B., is a well-published Benedictine monk and priest. He is also an academic: he specializes in moral theology and teaches at Saint Meinrad Seminary and School of Theology. This work clearly manifests his giftedness in communicating his ideas to others.

Father O'Keefe is no novice with regard to Carmelite spirituality. He notes his "passion for Teresa and for John of the Cross," has done specialized studies in Avila, and has taught courses on the two Carmelite Doctors of the Church. Furthermore, this is not his first book on Carmelite spirituality. His previous book with ICS Publications (2014), *Love Awakened by Love: The Liberating Ascent of St. John of the Cross*, has been awarded for excellence by the Catholic Press Association of the United States and Canada. In this present work, Father O'Keefe generously shares with us his investigations into Teresian spirituality, focusing particularly on the transformation of life brought about through the practice of prayer and the virtues.

Many people living in our Western, secularized, scientific, and technologized world, dominated by materialism and consumerism, yearn for "something more." The almost complete satisfaction of our bodily needs, so easily attainable today, has awakened us to the deeper spiritual needs within. This "something more" is often expressed as a "hunger for God" or a thirst for "spiritual experience." To this end, there has been a burgeoning of various forms of spiritualities—from the mainline Christian churches and world religions to New Age spiritualities—all promising peace and contentment through an experience of the divine. Carmelite spirituality—principally communicated in the writings of Saints Teresa and John of the Cross—also promises to show a way of connecting with the divine.

Of particular concern, however, is the fact that, while many are looking for transcendent prayer experiences or mystical phenomena, these are often sought as ends in themselves. In other words, in our affluent, materialistic and consumerist Western world, spirituality is too often sought as a form of therapy, and so is reduced to yet another self-actuating consumer product rather than a way of life with God and others. To express this tendency in more traditional terms, in our contemporary situation the *mystical* is often separated from the *ascetical*.

Being a moral theologian, with, as he notes, a "long interest in the relationship of spirituality and ethics," Father O'Keefe's focus in this work is on exploring Teresian Carmelite spirituality through the lens of moral theology, thereby holding together the mystical and ascetical dimensions of the spiritual life. In this respect, he offers a much-needed corrective for those who tend to unduly seek mystical phenomena, while neglecting the equally important ascetical aspects of the spiritual life.

St. Teresa is rightly associated with prayer and contemplative/mystical experiences. This is understandable, given the fact that she is accredited in the church as a mystic (that is, a person steeped in experience of the divine), and as a teacher/doctor of prayer (an authority able to articulate her experiences, and to guide others in the ways of prayer). Moreover, her major works offer a rich resource from which we can learn about the nature and journey of prayer, and also detail the extraordinary experiences attained in mystical/contemplative prayer. In this book, Father O'Keefe draws our attention to the not-so-well-known fact that undergirding St. Teresa's spirituality of prayer are the virtues.

For St. Teresa, prayer is primarily a personal relationship of intimate friendship with God, "the One who we know loves us." Although this relationship is initiated by God, growth in this friendship demands our cooperation. And as happens with any authentic relationship, with prayer, too, we are changed and transformed. In this respect, Father O'Keefe's work strongly accentuates the fact that prayer necessarily brings about personal transformation: "The journey of prayer is a journey of transformation."

Authentic friendships, however, are not without cost; they demand a secure foundation and personal investment if the relationship is to be kept alive and healthy. For St. Teresa, the personal investment and foundation for growth in prayer equate to virtuous living. The author alerts us to the fact that, for St. Teresa, prayer and the virtues are inseparable and complementary. They are two sides of the one reality. On the one hand, without prayer, growth in the virtues leading to a transformation of life is impossible; and, on the other hand, without growth in the virtues, prayer is illusory. Hence, transformation of life is necessarily the fruit of authentic prayer.

St. Teresa proposes three virtues—love of neighbor, detachment, and humility—as being foundational for growth in prayer, leading to personal transformation and the possibility of contemplation. Why "possibility"? Because, as Father O'Keefe points out, according to St. Teresa, contemplative experiences are not at our disposal or contrivance; they are sheer unmerited gift. While we can prepare ourselves to receive the gift of contemplation through fidelity to prayer and the exercise of the virtues, contemplation always remains God's prerogative. Furthermore, as St. Teresa reminds us, although contemplative/mystical experiences are certainly a boon on our spiritual journey, and are even to be welcomed with thanksgiving, they must not be selfishly sought after. These experiences are not necessary for salvation, nor are they necessarily indications of greater holiness. True holiness is evident only in the personal transformation brought about through the living of the virtues.

Father O'Keefe not only provides us with a masterful and comprehensive account of each of the three virtues within the context of Teresa's day, but, even more helpfully, he grounds them in contemporary life, demonstrating their applicability and relevance for us today. He also provides us with an insightful and fulsome account of the particularly Teresian attitude of "determination," which must nurture our resolve to do God's will, not our own will, at every stage of the spiritual journey. He points to the fact that, for Teresa, this attitude is so essential that it "can rightly be called the fourth necessary virtue."

There are many other topics that Father O'Keefe addresses in this exploration, such as St. Teresa's anthropology and the place of sin, her doctrine of prayer, and her use of the image of the silkworm to speak about spiritual transformation. Each of these engages and informs us about "the way of transformation."

This is a timely, practical, and welcome book on Teresian Carmelite spirituality from a Benedictine monk who has deeply pondered and prayed through the writings of St. Teresa of Avila. It is not only a work of information, but also a book of formation, assisting us to appropriate more deeply St. Teresa's spirituality. To this end, a challenging set of questions for personal reflection is provided for each chapter.

I certainly profited from reading *The Way of Transformation*, and am sure that it will similarly profit greatly all those who wish to acquaint themselves with the spirituality of St. Teresa of Avila, as well as those who are already her disciples.

Aloysius Rego, O.C.D.
Mt. Carmel Retreat Centre
Varroville, NSW
Australia

Introduction

S t. Teresa of Avila, mystic and Doctor of the Church, is undoubtedly one of the greatest teachers of prayer in the entire Christian tradition. All of her major works, in some way, offer rich teaching on prayer. Although she describes extraordinary experiences in prayer, they are not her principal focus. Her spiritual teaching is neither elitist nor a kind of "high spirituality" beyond the aspirations of ordinary people. Although she is considered one of the greatest mystics in the Christian tradition, her readers will find her to be very human, down to earth, and warm.

For Teresa of Jesus (as she is more properly called, according to the name she took at the beginning of the Carmelite reform), prayer is never cut off from our daily living. "The Lord," she reminds us, "walks among the pots and pans" (F 5.8). As the well-known expert on Carmelite spirituality Keith Egan assures us, Teresa knew well the truth that "we pray as well as we live and we live as well as we pray."[1] Prayer is intimately and necessarily linked with personal transformation. If we wish to grow in prayer, we must actively engage, with God's help, in the work of ongoing conversion. Only then can we become fertile ground for the gift of deepening prayer. At the same time, encounter and union with God inevitably bears fruit in a more profound transformation.

Teresa famously defined prayer as "an intimate sharing between friends; it means taking time frequently to be alone

---

1. Keith J. Egan, *Teresa, Teach Us to Pray*, Study Guide (Rockville, Md.: Now You Know Media, 2011), 11.

1

with Him who we know loves us" (L 8.5). Prayer is based in a relationship. It is an intimate exchange between friends. Less well known is the fact Teresa follows up immediately by saying, "In order that love be true and the friendship endure, the wills of the friends must be in accord." She tells us that we must work to conform ourselves more completely to God's loving will. Otherwise, "you will endure the pain of spending a long while with one who is so different from you when you see how much it benefits you to possess His friendship and how much He loves you." If prayer is an intimate exchange between friends, then we must become more like this divine friend if we hope for the friendship and the prayer to endure and grow. Growth in prayer is also a growth in divine friendship, and both require a foundation in how we live.

The journey of prayer is a journey of transformation. Teresa is not the first or the only voice that has proclaimed this fundamental truth. It is a mainstay of the Christian spiritual tradition—indeed of the spiritual traditions of all the major religions. But her teaching offers a voice of profound experience and insight that explores the Christian journey from its beginnings to its summit in union with God. The bond between prayer and transformation runs through her writing, and her spiritual wisdom cannot be fully understood without seeing this fundamental truth.

Teresa offers us the most explicit and extended discussion of the necessary foundation of prayer in a life of ongoing transformation in *The Way of Perfection*. This is the work that Kieran Kavanaugh, O.C.D., has called "Teresa's handbook for initial and ongoing spiritual formation" and "an education for contemplation."[2] Teresa sets out to teach the way of prayer to her nuns,

2. Teresa of Avila, *The Way of Perfection*, study ed., prepared by Kieran Kavanaugh, trans. Kieran Kavanaugh and Otilio Rodriguez (Washington, D.C.: ICS Publications, 2000), 1.

from its beginnings to its most advanced stages, but she spends the first half of the book explaining three essential virtues that are the foundation of any real growth in prayer. Clearly, there is no point in speaking of advancing in prayer without an explanation of its indispensable foundation. In *The Interior Castle* too, in which Teresa lays out the progress of prayer through the image of a journey through seven dwelling places, she addresses this same essential foundation, though in less detail, especially in the first three of the dwelling places (IC 2.1.1).[3]

Perhaps it would be natural enough to want to pass over any close study of this necessary foundation in living in order to arrive quickly at the teaching on contemplative prayer. Maybe her first readers felt the same way. One commentator tells us that it appears Teresa feared that her first readers were preoccupied with the *exercise* of prayer, while she was concerned with a *life* of prayer—or with the person who prays.[4] The truth is that Teresa is not merely offering some optional advice in her teaching on the three virtues explained in *The Way of Perfection* and on the effort to form them securely within us. No, she says they are essential. And, although she devotes less attention to the first three dwellings of *The Interior Castle* that focus on the same general foundation, she clearly does not mean to suggest that these first dwellings are in any way optional or unimportant. We simply cannot, without some special and rare intervention of God, arrive at the fourth dwellings where contemplation begins without passing through these first three dwellings. The transformation of our manner of living, together with faithful attention

---

3. Teresa says that she had already addressed the early stages elsewhere. Kavanaugh associates this statement with chapters 11 through 13 of *The Book of Her Life* and with *The Way of Perfection* more generally. Kieran Kavanaugh and Carol Lisi, *The Interior Castle*, study ed. (Washington, D.C.: ICS Publications, 2010), 65n111.

4. Maximiliano Herráiz, *Introducción al Camino de Perfección* (Burgos, Spain: Editorial Monte Carmelo, 2001), 71.

to our prayer, is indispensable. Growth in prayer requires the remaking of the person who prays, and at the same time, the person is remade as a fruit of prayer.[5]

In Teresa's own day, it might have been possible to say that there were many books about the ascetical or liberating stages that prepare the fertile ground for the gift of contemplative prayer (IC 2.1.1). And so, at least in *The Interior Castle*, she could pass relatively quickly through them in order to speak about "supernatural" prayer. But in our own day, it may be that the opposite is true. There are many books on prayer but few that examine the transformation that is essential for deepening prayer. There are, of course, ample fine texts on the Christian moral life in general, focusing these days on discussion of the virtues. That discussion is essential too. But what Teresa is speaking of in the first half of *The Way of Perfection* offers a more particular focus on the liberating or transformative efforts that provide the bridge between our moral lives properly speaking and the preparation for contemplative prayer.

In pre–Vatican II theology, there was an academic discipline of moral theology that looked at moral acts, laws, and to some degree virtues. In what we would today call the study of spirituality, there was the discipline of ascetical and mystical theology, sometimes explicitly divided into separate studies of the ascetical and the mystical. Ascetical theology focused on virtue, but not on the kind of virtues that we build up by our own graced efforts, which today are properly the focus of moral theology. Rather it focused on "infused" virtues, that is, the abiding dispositions to the good that are given by God in order to direct our lives to God. And so, ascetical theology taught about the personal transformation, empowered by God

---

5. Teresa of Avila, *Way of Perfection*, 74.

with our active cooperation, that is necessary for contemplative prayer (the focus of mystical theology).

There are many reasons not to return to the division of moral, ascetical, and mystical theology taught before the Second Vatican Council. It was, for example, inherently elitist. It was assumed, if not actually taught, that moral theology was for the ordinary Christians who needed to say their prayers, go to Mass and confession, and follow the commandments. Ascetical and mystical theology were perceived to be for the elite—for priests and religious (and perhaps not even for all of them). It is a wonderful development that contemporary spirituality is egalitarian, incarnational, and more biblical—just to mention a few positive contemporary developments. But I do think that something is lost in the relative lack of attention to some of the subject matter of the old ascetical theology (as much as it might need updating in relation to other developments in theology). What is often lost is what Teresa is addressing in speaking of the three essential virtues in *The Way of Perfection* and in laying out the first three dwellings of *The Interior Castle*. She is not speaking of morality as such, nor are the virtues on which she focuses the principal moral virtues. She is speaking of a deeper transformation and liberation of our freedom in order to truly receive God's love fully and to love God in return.

What Teresa offers us, in traditional terms, is an entire ascetical and mystical theology. This is not to say that it is systematic. But it is a view of the entire Christian journey from its beginnings to its most profound depths offered by someone who walked the entire path herself. And on that journey, she reflected, consulted, read, and received divine assistance to understand and to explain the way. Today, many are justifiably most interested in what would be called her mystical theology, but her entire work—and its continuing value for us today—cannot be fully understood without also giving attention to what would be called her ascetical theology. Her way of transformation, as I am calling it, is not the entire picture (that is, without a more thorough discussion of her teaching on prayer than I will offer here), but it is an essential—and too easily neglected—part of it.

To ignore or to pass too quickly over Teresa's teaching on the transformation essential for prayer to grow is to neglect what this Doctor of the Church and great teacher of prayer says is necessary. It is to pass over as well what the Christian spiritual tradition has taught since the early centuries of the church. We cannot be fertile ground for contemplation unless we transform our lives with the help of God's grace. To examine with care and understand Teresa's teaching on this transformation—and why in her own context she taught as she did—is to understand and hopefully embrace the work of human and divine cooperation that simply cannot be bypassed or short-circuited. The lives and teaching of the great mystics of the Christian tradition—in which St. Teresa stands as a great example—make this abundantly clear.

The ongoing transformation of life—motivations, attitudes, behaviors, and relationships—is the foundation of prayer, but it is equally true that all authentic prayer bears fruit in life transformation. With the description of virtually every prayerful encounter with God, Teresa reports some fruit that it has borne in her life, whether, for example, in greater love, detachment, or humility. Although our own efforts at an ever deeper and more thorough conversion seem to predominate in the earlier stages of growth in the Christian life and prayer, these efforts themselves are always the result of grace at work and our response to grace. Prayer at every stage bears fruit in our living. And while the gift of contemplative prayer and union results in yet more growth, we must at every stage embrace and cooperate with God's work of making us new. In what follows, we will be focusing especially on *our* graced work of transformation as the foundation for growth in prayer. But the truth is that our efforts and God's grace and the fruit it bears go hand in hand. We will see how Teresa herself was fully aware of this divine-human partnership—of which we are most definitely the junior members.

The present book then does not focus its principal attention on Teresa's classic teaching on prayer, though her work cannot be understood without attending to it. The late Ernest Larkin, O.Carm., noted that the key disciplines for growth in prayer according to Teresa are charity, detachment, and humility. Together with prayer, he argued, the four collectively are constitutive elements of a vibrant spiritual life. They are both the means for and the outcomes of spiritual growth. Larkin then makes the intriguing suggestion that these four elements could be studied in different configurations—focusing more attention on one rather than the other, while still holding them together. While Teresa's spirituality centers on prayer without neglect of the other three elements, Larkin maintained that there is no reason that her teaching could not be understood through the focus of one or the other element.[6] I have no intention of trying to suggest that prayer is not Teresa's principal focus, but I do want to suggest that in the "mix" of these four elements there is real value in examining her project from the perspective of the other three elements, which together I am calling both instruments and fruits of transformation.

Perhaps this is the most appropriate perspective for an author trained as an academic moral theologian, with long interest in

---

6. Ernest E. Larkin, "Human Relationships in Saint Teresa of Avila," in *The Land of Carmel: Essays in Honor of Joachim Smet, O.Carm.*, ed. Paul Chandler and Keith J. Egan, 285–97 (Rome: Institutum Carmelitanum, 1991). I accessed the article from "The Published Articles of Ernest E. Larkin, O.Carm.," Carmel Net, accessed December 17, 2015, http://www.carmelnet.org/larkin/larkin032.pdf, 142.

the relationship of spirituality and ethics. It is my hope that I can bring a distinctive lens to a full, contemporary understanding of the spiritual teaching of this Doctor of the Church. Surely, like her first readers, many of us would like to focus quickly and even exclusively on prayer. But she herself insists that, in living her teaching and in following her way, this is just not possible. Perhaps the viewpoint of a moral theologian looking through the lens of life transformation can help us to see why this is so.

The title of this book, *The Way of Transformation*, is a play on the title of Teresa's *The Way of Perfection* (though I do not intend to offer a commentary on that work nor to take it as my only focus). By speaking of "perfection," Teresa does not intend to suggest the futile attempt to pursue some idealized flawlessness. As we will see, she teaches that even in the seventh dwelling places we remain capable of imperfections and even venial sins. Rather, she means an authentic human fulfillment—a true becoming of who we were meant to be. And, for Teresa, this can only be found in conformity to God's will and in divine union. The way to that perfection is necessarily a way of transformation.

Our exploration into Teresa's teaching on transformation and prayer will draw on both *The Way of Perfection* and *The Interior Castle* (and to a lesser degree, on other of her works). Doing so, it must also be noted that Teresa is not a systematic writer, nor did she have a formal theological or literary education (which is not to say that this Doctor of the Church was not a great theologian). She wrote as she could find time between her many activities, her thoughts developing over time with her experience. Still, these factors do not prevent an essential consistency in her writings, and it is this consistency that will allow us to draw together the teachings of these two classic works without implying that we could simply paste them together as if there were no development between them.

We begin our study of Teresa's work by looking first at the journey of transformation as a whole, using the framework provided by *The Interior Castle*, which sees the Christian itinerary as a passage through seven dwelling places.

In the second chapter, again drawing on *The Interior Castle*, we will look more closely at the beginning of this journey. Teresa tells us that we begin the journey and enter the castle of our souls through the door of prayer and self-knowledge—neither of which is necessarily easy. Looking at ourselves, what we see is both tremendous beauty and the ugly reality of sin. Fundamentally, though, Teresa has a profoundly positive view of the human person created in the image of God. And so, despite the presence of sin, which cannot be ignored, our transforming journey is not based on a need to overcome some basic wretchedness at the core of our humanity. It is instead a kind of becoming what we already are. Our task, with God's help, is to recover and embrace what is truly good in us and allow God to "perfect" it through divine union.

In *The Way of Perfection*, Teresa tells us that we must practice and develop three essential virtues if we hope to grow in prayer. In chapter 3, we will first look at these virtues together as tools for an inner liberation to respond more completely to God's love. And, since they are together instruments for laying the foundation for deeper prayer, we will also summarize her teaching on the journey of prayer in this context. We will then examine the three virtues individually in chapters 4 through 6 as they appear in Teresa's teaching and in their contemporary importance. The great teacher of prayer tells us that we must walk the path of prayer and transformation with a "very determined determination," and so in chapter 7 we will look at this resolute persistence in her life and in our own.

In chapter 8, we will turn our main focus from transformation *for* deeper prayer to transformation as a *fruit* of contemplation and union. Teresa's works are full of her own experience of these fruits. As we shall see, she often focuses more attention on the effects of prayer than on detailed description of spiritual experiences that are ultimately ineffable—unable to be adequately described, understood, or explained.

By way of conclusion, we will examine a central image that Teresa uses for transformation: the silkworm that weaves a cocoon, dies in it, and is transformed into a beautiful butterfly. Through this rich metaphor, she teaches us about both our own graced efforts and God's gratuitous work in our lives.

In the year 2015, we celebrated the 500th anniversary of the birth of this amazing woman and Doctor of the Church. We see perhaps more clearly that it is time to discover, to encounter once again, or to enter more deeply into the virtually unsurpassed insights that St. Teresa of Avila offers to us, to the church, and to all of those who are seekers of God. Let us begin then, calling on her prayers and seeking to follow her along the way of transformation by which we can hope to receive the gift of contemplation—and, having received it, allow it to bear still greater fruit in our lives and in the world.

Translations and Abbreviations

Scripture quotations are from the *New Revised Standard Version Bible, Catholic Edition, Anglicized Text*, copyright ©1999, 1995, 1989, Division of Christian Education of the National Council of Churches of Christ of the United States of America. Used with permission. All rights reserved.

All quotations from the works of Teresa of Avila are taken from *The Collected Works of St. Teresa of Avila*, trans. Kieran Kavanaugh, O.C.D., and Otilio Rodriguez, O.C.D., 3 vols. (Washington, D.C.: ICS Publications, 1976–1985, 1987, 2012).

The following abbreviations will be used in references to Teresa's works:

F = *The Book of the Foundations*
L = *The Book of Her Life*
M = *Meditations on the Song of Songs*
W = *The Way of Perfection*
IC = *The Interior Castle*
Ltr = *Letters*
Sol = *Soliloquies*
ST = *Spiritual Testimonies*

For the first four works, the first number refers to the chapter, and the second number refers to the paragraph. Thus, W 3.5 refers to *The Way of Perfection*, chapter 3, paragraph 5. Regarding *The Interior Castle*, the first number refers to the dwelling place, the second number refers to the chapter, and the third number refers to the paragraph. Thus, IC 3.4.2 refers to the third dwelling place, chapter 4, paragraph 2.

1

—— ⚜ ——

THE PATH OF TRANSFORMATION: THE BIG PICTURE

I n *The Interior Castle*, the most mature of Teresa's major works, we see the spiritual life as a whole within the structure of one overarching image. Let us imagine, she says, that the soul is like a great castle. It contains what we can picture as seven concentric layers of dwelling places, with God dwelling in the inmost chamber.[1] God calls us to divine union at this deepest center, and so we must journey through the seven dwellings, more and more dependent on the help of grace. In the first three dwellings in this great journey, our own efforts seem to predominate as we seek to make ourselves fertile ground for the gift of contemplation. In the remaining four, it is God who is increasingly the agent. We become, as is traditionally said, more "passive" (though the words "docile" or "receptive" might better capture the reality for us today). And as God gives the gift of deepening union, the encounters with God bear increasing fruit in the person's living.

Teresa's classic image of the interior castle and the panoramic view of the spiritual life that it provides helps us to place her teaching on transformation in her own framework. In fact, Teresa devotes significantly less attention to the first three

---

1. "Dwelling places" translates the Spanish term *moradas*, probably more accurately capturing Teresa's image than the other traditional English translation, "mansions."

dwelling places. It seems that she was anxious to get to her teaching on contemplation for the sake of her nuns and others who would have had few other resources to help them navigate the new world of contemplation.[2] Indeed, she had already taught about the necessary ascetical preparation in the first half of her earlier work on prayer, *The Way of Perfection*. For that reason, in many of the chapters that follow here, we will focus our attention on her teaching in the *Way*. But as we begin it will be useful to look at the big picture provided by *The Interior Castle*. And, in the next chapter, still drawing on the *Castle*, we will see more particularly how Teresa came to understand the journey's starting point and first steps.

THE INTERIOR CASTLE

> We consider our soul to be like a castle made entirely out of a diamond or very clear crystal, in which there are many rooms, just as in heaven there are many dwelling places. . . . some up above, others down below, others to the sides; and in the center and middle is the main dwelling place where the very secret exchanges between God and the soul take place. (IC 1.1.1, 3)

Kieran Kavanaugh, O.C.D., suggests that the image of the soul as a castle is grounded in a vision that Teresa recounts in the final chapter of *The Book of Her Life*: her soul as a brightly polished mirror with Christ at its very center but filling every part of it (L 40.5–6).[3] This vision may have come to her mind as she asked

---

2. The Inquisition had placed on the index of forbidden books virtually every book in Spanish that dealt with the prayer of recollection or contemplation—for fear of leading pious Christians into error. Teresa describes this event and its effect on her in *The Book of Her Life*, 26.5.

3. Teresa of Avila, *The Collected Works of St. Teresa of Avila*, trans. Kieran Kavanaugh and Otilio Rodriguez, rev. ed. (Washington, D.C.: ICS Publications, 1987), 1:490n6.

the Lord to help her to begin the writing of *The Interior Castle* (IC 1.1.1). Kavanaugh also sees this vision as the basis for one of the most beautiful chapters in *The Way of Perfection* (W 28.9–12), in which Teresa invites her readers to imagine within them "an extremely rich palace" in which dwells a mighty king. There, she expressed her wonder: "For in my opinion, if I had understood as I do now that in this little palace of my soul dwelt so great a King, I would not have left him alone so often. I would have remained with Him at all times and striven more so as not to be so unclean. But what a marvelous thing, that He who would fill a thousand worlds and many more with His grandeur would enclose Himself in something so small!" (W 28.11).

It should be noted that it would be difficult to lay out diagrammatically the structure of this interior castle. On the one hand, it is a castle with a clear exterior and a distinct interior. What is exterior to the castle represents temptation and superficiality (though the image does not mean to suggest that everything outside the human person is evil), and this is a castle with walls that are meant to protect and to serve in warfare (rather than, generally, a "palace"). The dwelling places within the castle are arranged concentrically around the innermost chamber in which the divine King dwells. It is difficult to picture this arrangement literally—dwellings arranged concentrically within castle walls—just as it is difficult to imagine that each dwelling place consists of many rooms above, below, and around, through which the soul might pass (IC 1.2.8; IC Epi.3).[4] In fact, Teresa tells us at one point that we should think in terms of not a few rooms in each of the dwelling places but a million of them! (IC 1.2.12)

---

4. It has been suggested that some approximation of Teresa's image might be found in an aerial view of the U.S. Pentagon.

The image of the castle with its many rooms provides an overarching framework for Teresa, but she is telling us that the experience of each individual will be distinctive within a broadly envisioned itinerary. God seeks relationship with us and invites us into union as unique individuals. Teresa is not suggesting that we march directly, in lockstep fashion, through a clearly marked path that is one-size-fits-all. In fact, we might recognize ourselves in the descriptions of more than one of the dwelling places. It might seem that we have one foot in one dwelling and the other foot in another. We might feel ourselves moving between one or the other or suspect that Teresa has not fully captured our experience even though her description of a particular dwelling place seems to fit us more generally. I suspect that Teresa would have expected as much. Our purpose here is simply to provide a broad overview of what we are calling Teresa's way of transformation— a framework for what will follow—and so, for that purpose, we will simply (perhaps a bit simplistically) lay out the progression of the dwelling places as Teresa has described it.

The First Dwellings

Following Teresa's spatial image of the journey through the castle, the first dwellings are the most exterior and thus the farthest away from the innermost chamber from which emanates the true light. In these outermost dwellings, then, we would enjoy little light. Or, as Teresa describes it in another way, even the outermost room is in fact bright with the divine light, but it is as if we were so distracted and even blinded by superficialities (which she calls vermin and poisonous creatures)—or as if we had our eyes closed to the light—that we cannot see the light of God's presence even though it is brilliantly shining. These "superficialities" for Teresa are all the things that are not necessarily evil in themselves but which lack ultimate value—such as unnecessary possessions, mere appearances, worldly status, and honor. These things have only passing value at best, but we can all too easily invest them with greater importance than they merit in relation to the ultimate meaning and purpose of our lives.

While we would have stepped into the interior castle, in these outer dwellings we would still be distracted and tempted by what we have experienced outside. We might make some time for prayer, but much of our focus would still be on the possessions, honors, and business of life outside. We might not be in a "bad state" in the sense of serious sin, but we would remain "easily conquered"; and, in these first dwellings, we remain in constant danger of being "bitten" by these poisonous creatures (IC 1.2.10–14).

> Teresa is not suggesting that we march directly, in lockstep fashion, through a clearly marked path that is one-size-fits-all.

The challenge for those in the first dwellings is, according to their "state in life," to give up their excessive focus on or attachment to trivial and unnecessary things. Teresa already begins to refer to the tools or weapons that will be necessary to continue this inward movement—things such as self-knowledge and humility, detachment, and the practical love of others rather than selfish pursuits. These are instruments that will continue to be essential along the way (as well as, at the same time, being fruits of a deepening prayer and openness to the action of God). And these instruments will be the focus of the following chapters of this book. Threatened as people are in these first dwellings, or outer chambers, so ready to be enticed to return to life outside the interior castle, they must constantly seek the help of God and the intercession of the Blessed Mother and the saints.

A fundamental challenge of the first dwellings is to discover the marvelous dignity of the human soul and to discover one's own interiority—and, at the same time, to discover that God dwells at very center of this interiority. With these first steps, the Christian must begin to see the basic challenge and, at least in an initial way, the obstacles that lie ahead.

The Second Dwellings

The first and only chapter on the second dwelling places begins with this title: "Discusses the importance of perseverance if one is to reach the final dwelling places." Perseverance or determination is a central theme in Teresa's work, but here her purpose is simply to make clear that once we have each entered into our own interior castle, we must work hard, with God's help, to stay there and to make progress.

In the second dwellings, we have taken the first steps inward and have begun a practice of prayer and drawing help from good sermons, books, and devotions; but people in these dwellings often do not avoid the occasions of sin that could all too easily draw them out. It is almost as if we had been bitten by one of those poisonous creatures (attachments to what is only of passing value), and this deadly wound continues to afflict and to threaten us. This is the reason for the utter necessity of perseverance and constant appeal to God's help.

Still, the merciful God, dwelling within and desiring greatly that we love in return, continuously calls out, and we have begun to listen. We have begun to be truly awakened to the love that God has shown to us individually and to all. Faith has been awakened to God as friend and lover. We begin to see the true futility and superficiality of the things that we used to love so wholeheartedly and that continue even here to call us back.

Again introducing an important theme of her work, Teresa warns that we must not expect or even seek after consolations—warm and consoling feelings of God's presence and favor—at this stage: "These are not the dwelling places where it rains manna." With a typical irony, she notes how "amusing" it is to see that we who are only beginning and so far from attaining and conforming our lives to God think of making demands and complaining to God that we are not being given continual sweetness in our prayer.

Part of the determination here is the necessity of not giving into discouragement. We have not yet arrived at the inmost dwellings, but we have begun. We have taken the first steps. God can draw good out of our falls, and such failings can make us more aware of our weakness, our need, and the importance of remaining vigilant. Echoing the thought of St. Paul that "all things work together for good for those who love God" (Rom 8:28), Teresa says, "Provided that we don't give up, the Lord will guide everything for our benefit" (IC 2.1.10).

The theme of perseverance and determination, which we will discuss at greater length in a future chapter, calls to mind the battle images that Teresa often uses here and elsewhere. The title of this great work involves a castle—a fortress, a bastion against an enemy. The title of the chapter devoted to the second dwellings speaks of the "great war" that the devil wages. "Let the soul always heed the warning not to be conquered," she urges, and be like soldiers going into battle "determined to fight with all the devils and realize that there are no better weapons than those of the cross" (IC 2.1.6). We must be like the three hundred valiant soldiers of Gideon (Jgs 7:4–6) who did not flee but prepared to face the considerably larger Midianite army.

In fact, the city of Avila, to this day, is surrounded by massive medieval walls, calling to mind the city's history as "*Ávila de los caballeros*" (of the knights). The image of the city in which she spent her early life and the stories of valiant knights that she loved to read as a child must have influenced her and fired her imagination. But for Teresa, the image of the castle and other militaristic images point to the fact that the inward journey through these inner dwellings is not a casual stroll. The journey requires struggle, determination, and commitment—a kind of fundamental option ("*una opción radical*"), as one noted commentator has said.[5] The disorder of sin and its continuing power must be confronted and overcome, and this struggle is not accomplished at one moment so that we can simply move on. No, the struggle goes deeper, to uproot more deeply entrenched attachments and disorder. We have all lived under the tyranny of superficiality from outside, and so we must engage with resolution in the struggle to overcome that slavery and gain our inner freedom and self-dominion in God.[6]

The Third Dwellings

God has blessed people greatly to have brought them through their ongoing struggle to these third dwellings. In fact, they are what we would recognize as "good" and solid Christians: "They long not to offend His Majesty, even guarding themselves against venial sins; they are fond of penance and setting aside periods for recollection; they spend their time well, practicing works of charity toward their neighbors; and are very balanced in their use of speech and dress and in governing their households—those

---

5. Tomás Alvarez, *Comentarios a las obras de Santa Teresa: Libro de la vida, Camino de perfección, Castillo interior* (Burgos, Spain: Editorial Monte Carmelo, 2005), 570.

6. Ibid., 575.

who have them" (IC 3.1.5). If such persons desire it and remain faithful in their determination, there is every reason to believe that God will give them that which they desire and for which they strive.

Beyond a general statement about the people who have reached these dwellings, Teresa seems to say little more directly about the specific challenges of this stage except for the danger of feeling secure in one's journey, the need to resist the desire for consolations, and the need for humility and continued detachment. Nonetheless, Teresa is suggesting in these challenges that the struggle has now gone deeper. The focus, one commentator has noted, is liberation from self-deception, selfishness, and narcissism in order to truly love and to become what one truly is in the depths of oneself.[7] In the desire for spiritual consolations, we only demonstrate that attachment to the superficial runs far deeper than the material things to which we could be attached. We can also become attached to shallow (and perhaps false) experience in prayer and thus fashion a false god who can satisfy our craving for good feelings in prayer but who is, by no means, the God whom we should be seeking. And Teresa's response to this challenge is, "Oh, humility, humility!" (IC 3.1.7), for we must let the one true God decide about consolation or dryness. We must humbly allow God to lead us according to the divine will, not according to our selfishness.

The Fourth Dwellings

The fourth dwelling places represent the transition from the active stage of prayer, in which our activity and discipline seem primary, into the experience of "infused" (receptive or passive)

---

7. Ibid., 580–81.

prayer. The passage then is from vocal prayers, heartfelt devotions, spiritual reading, active meditation (i.e., prayerful reflection and the active use of the imagination in prayer)—and even from the disciplined practice of an "active" recollection—to the first experiences of true contemplative prayer.[8] In these fourth dwellings, contemplation begins with the gift of "infused" recollection in which God gathers and quiets the faculties. Prayer thus moves from our human action to pure divine gift.

Clearly, it is precisely the prior, sustained effort to rid ourselves of attachments and to overcome the tyranny of superficiality that lays the necessary groundwork for this transition. We arrive at these dwellings only after entering the interior castle by prayer, struggling with determination to stay within, resisting the temptations to be pulled back out, and growing in the interior attitudes of detachment and humility. Here begins the stage in which what becomes most important for us is "not to think much but to love much" (IC 4.1.7).

The Fifth Dwellings

The prayer of union with God, at least in a relatively brief and occasional way, is characteristic of the fifth dwellings. Here, Teresa introduces the language of courtship and marriage to describe the union of the soul with God. In the fifth dwellings, it is as though God and the soul are engaged in a formal courtship, coming together occasionally to know one another more deeply and to grow into a truer love. We must continue our preparation and intensify our self-giving to God in love: "Whether you have little or much, He wants everything for Himself" (IC 5.1.3). This metaphor for deepening union will continue with

---

8. We will look more closely at Teresa's terminology for prayer in chapter 3.

the spiritual betrothal of the sixth dwellings and the spiritual marriage of the seventh.

From images of inner journey and struggle, in chapter 2 of the fifth dwellings, Teresa introduces as well the image of a silkworm and cocoon. The silkworm, fat and ugly, begins to spin the silk with which it will form a cocoon and in which it will then enclose itself. There within the cocoon, it will die, only to emerge as a pretty, white butterfly. This is a wonderful image of transformation that we will examine more closely later. At this point, it is important to recognize that Teresa is using it here to suggest a more profound transformation of the person as he or she enters into deeper experiences of union with God.

In these fifth dwellings, as elsewhere, Teresa links prayer and transformation with love. The most perfect sign that one has truly experienced union with God is its essential fruit, love of neighbor: "When you see yourselves lacking in this love [of neighbor], even though you have devotion and gratifying experiences that make you think that you have reached this stage, and you experience some little suspension in the prayer of quiet (for to some it then appears that everything has been accomplished), believe me you have not reached union. And beg our Lord to give you this perfect love of neighbor" (IC 5.3.12). Love as a fruit of prayer will become even clearer in the description of the seventh dwellings.

The Sixth Dwellings

Teresa's description of the sixth dwelling places is the longest of *The Interior Castle*. It includes her account of many forms of extraordinary mystical phenomena that, she explains, are manifestations of the lack of accommodation between the spirit and the body, between the divine and human. Since we are both spirit and body together, the inflow or closeness of God and union with the divine unsettles the body, requiring a period of accommodation or adjustment. It is true, as we will explain in the next chapter, that we are created in the image of God and therefore we are made for union with God (as a "capacity" for God). At the same time, we are still sinners and flesh and blood, and therefore limited. The infinite distance between God and our creaturely and sinful humanity must be bridged—at first by our graced effort but increasingly and essentially by God's gracious gift and action. Here, in the penultimate dwellings, the final accommodations or adjustments result in phenomena that overwhelm human consciousness: visions, ecstasies, and raptures. When concluding the account of *The Book of Her Life*, some fifteen years before she completed *The Interior Castle*, Teresa had thought that such phenomena represented the final stages of the spiritual journey. As she explains here in her mature masterpiece, such experiences are a sublime and extraordinary stage through which one may pass, though not exactly in the same way for all.

Here, in the sixth dwellings, continuing the imagery of courtship and marriage, Teresa tells us that the soul enters into spiritual betrothal. The experiences of union deepen so that they overflow into the exterior faculties and senses. We are filled with desire and yearning for full union—"wounded" with love. We long for the divine spark in the soul to become an all-consuming blaze, even as an interior confidence grows within it.

The mystical phenomena of the sixth dwellings, as Teresa experienced them, are both exquisite and painful—and, at first, frightening. The encounter with the divine presence and the love that comes with union is both sublime and torturous because, though profound and deep, they remain passing. In fact, the sixth dwelling places are, for Teresa, a passage through great suffering.

Here, at the threshold of the inmost chamber of the interior castle, there are not only the extraordinary phenomena that are the
result of the ongoing accommodation of the human to the inflow
of the divine. There is also the further and deeper liberating work
of purification that Teresa compares to the suffering of the souls in
purgatory as they prepare to pass into the divine union of heaven
(IC 6.11.6). The depths of the person must be stripped of what is
not God and of what is not compatible with union with God. We
shall examine this painful passage more closely in the final chapter, but the sixth dwellings as described by Teresa cannot be understood without reference to it.

Toward the end of her description of the sixth dwellings,
Teresa briefly reverses the image of the interior castle in which
God dwells to suggest that we imagine God as "an immense and
beautiful dwelling or palace" that contains everything within it
(IC 6.10.3).[9] In fact, the two images are necessary to provide a
broader sense of the immanence and the transcendence of God.
God dwells within us but is not contained by us. God is always
infinitely beyond us and yet intimately present to and within us.

The Seventh Dwellings

Teresa herself experienced the entry into the seventh and innermost chamber where God dwells with a vision of the Blessed
Trinity. In these inmost dwellings, the person abides in the
Persons of the Trinity. Here then the soul attains the spiritual
marriage, true abiding union with God. The experience of this
union no longer comes and goes. Though it is experienced more
or less intensely, the person lives in profound union with God in

---

9. In *The Book of Her Life*, Teresa briefly describes the vision that is the basis of this insight
(L 40.9).

the midst of the daily activities and responsibilities of his or her state in life. Gone are the extraordinary phenomena. The soul and body are conformed to the abiding presence of God.

In spiritual betrothal, Teresa says that the union of the soul and God is like the flames of two candles that are brought together for a time and thus burn together as one but are then separated once again into separate flames. On the other hand, in the spiritual marriage of the seventh dwellings, the union is like the waters of a stream that run into the sea, becoming one with it. Having offered this image, Teresa is quick to insist that in this union there is distinction without separation. We are not completely lost in God. Even in the most intimate union of this life and the next, we will continue to be ourselves even as we participate in the inner life of God (IC 7.2.4). More biblically, Teresa quotes St. Paul: "He that is joined or united to the Lord becomes one spirit with him" (1 Cor 6:17), and "For me to live is Christ, and to die is gain" (Phil 1:21). The little butterfly, which had come to life with the death of the ugly silkworm in the cocoon that is Christ, now dies, and its very life is Christ (IC 7.2.5).

This, at last, is the inmost chamber of the interior castle of the soul. The union of God and the human person "takes place in the very interior center of the soul" (IC 7.2.3). From that moment, the "soul always remains with its God in that center" (IC 7.2.4). The soul does not move from this union and so it never loses its peace, regardless of what is going on around it or the activity and bustle in which it is engaged (IC 7.2.6).

In the end, it is God who places us in this dwelling, in this place where the divine presence dwells: "The Lord puts the soul in this dwelling of His, which is the center of the soul itself" (IC 7.2.9). God is the agent of this entry into the center (IC 7.1.5). It is only God who can bring the human into its own deepest reality, because its deepest reality can be found only in God.

One might have expected that arrival at union with God in the center of the soul would bring Teresa's account to an end; but instead, having entered into spiritual marriage, we are challenged to engage in practical works of love for others: "This is the reason for prayer, my daughters, the purpose of the spiritual marriage: the birth always of good works, good works" (IC 7.4.6). In union with God, we become a divine instrument of love in the world. In images that may appear extreme to our modern sensitivities, Teresa says that since we have been branded with the cross, having given over our liberty, we must become slaves of God for the service of others (IC 7.4.8). United with God who is love, seeing the world and everything in it from within that union, we can only love our sisters and brothers. Or to say it another way, having been transformed in God, we discover the profound roots of our communion with others and so must reach out to serve them with God's own love to which we are united. The important thing here, Teresa assures us, is not the greatness of our works but the love with which we do them (IC 7.4.15).

2

THE JOURNEY BEGINS

The way of transformation as taught by Teresa of Jesus begins with wonder at the beauty of the human person created in the image of God, and it ends, in this life, with a transforming union with God. Every step of the way is empowered by God's grace, made possible by and as a response to the outpouring of divine love. At the same time, there is considerable effort on our own part that is required to liberate our freedom so that we can truly receive God's self-offering and love as we are being loved. There is the reality of sin—our sinful actions and attitudes, certainly. But there are the roots of sin that live more deeply within us, keeping us enslaved to self, to superficialities that are infinitely less than God, and to a possessiveness of others. As we set out to look more closely at the work of transformation, it is important to see how Teresa understands the beginning of this journey.

THE BEAUTY OF THE SOUL

I don't find anything comparable to the magnificent beauty of a soul and its marvelous capacity. Indeed, our intellects, however keen, can hardly comprehend it, just as they cannot comprehend God; but He Himself says that He created us in His own image and likeness. (IC 1.1.1)

The human soul of the just person, says Teresa, is "a paradise where the Lord says He finds His delight" (IC 1.1.1). With this insight, Teresa begins her reflection on the journey through this marvelous interior castle by observing the great beauty of the soul. The human soul—that is, the human person especially in his or her spiritual dimension—is a wonderful creation of God. Although we are "mere" creatures, we are wondrously made in the image of the divine. Teresa is filled with awe at this reality. Because we reflect the divinity so profoundly, she says it is "almost impossible for us to understand the sublime dignity and beauty of the soul."

In beginning her work this way, Teresa grounds all that follows on a profoundly positive perspective on our humanity. The human person is sublimely and almost inexpressibly precious by nature, and so, the way of transformation that Teresa will describe is not motivated by the need to escape or erase some inherent human wickedness. There is nothing authentic in our humanity that must be denied, ignored, or left behind on the path to union with God. Teresa herself demonstrates this truth with her own life—as her varied friendships and her lively letters filled with humor and the full range of human emotion make clear.

The path of our ongoing conversion and inner liberation is part of becoming what we were truly meant to be—and what, deep within every person, we still are. Our journey is a continuing effort, empowered by grace, to uproot sin within ourselves in order to become what God made us to be. And what God created us to be is the divine image—like God and in communion with God. In this sense, *The Interior Castle* is not only a book on deepening prayer but also a reflection on the deep and wonderful mystery and authentic development of the human person.[1]

---

1. Tomás Alvarez, *Comentarios a las obras de Santa Teresa: Libro de la vida, Camino de perfección, Castillo interior* (Burgos, Spain: Editorial Monte Carmelo, 2005), 541.

"Christian, remember your dignity!" Teresa's invitation to follow the path that leads to the restoration and perfection of what God has made us to be reflects this patristic call. We must remember who and what we are, and then we must live and act accordingly. The *Catechism of the Catholic Church* in beginning its discussion of the Christian moral life quotes a famous sermon of St. Leo the Great: "Christian, recognize your dignity and, now that you share in God's own nature, do not return to your former base condition by sinning. Remember who is your head and of whose body you are a member. Never forget that you have been rescued from the power of darkness and brought into the light of the Kingdom of God" (CCC, 1691).

> Precisely because we are created in the image of God and made for God, Teresa tells us that we will never know ourselves and become our truest selves unless we come to know God.

Teresa's call might be, "Christian, remember the beauty of your soul! Remember in whose image you have been so wondrously made!" The starting point of our journey of transformation is not the ugly reality of sin but the wondrous truth of our sublime dignity in God!

Precisely because we are created in the image of God and made for God, Teresa tells us that we will never know ourselves and become our truest selves unless we come to know God: "In my opinion we shall never completely know ourselves if we don't strive to know God" (IC 1.2.9). Because we are made in God's image, we must know God and become like God. Because God is love, we must love. Because we are created as a dwelling place for God, we must search for God within and remove every obstacle to the fullness of the divine presence. Because we are made for union with God, we must set out to prepare the ground of our lives so that God can pour the divine life on and into us.

MARRED BY SIN

In the first chapter of the first dwelling places of *The Interior Castle*, Teresa exults in the beauty of the human soul created in the image of God. In the second chapter, she confronts the reality of sin: "Consider what it would mean to this so brilliantly shining and beautiful castle, this pearl from the Orient, this tree of life planted in the very living waters of life—that is, in God—to fall into mortal sin; there's no darker darkness nor anything more obscure and black" (IC 1.2.1). In a similar way, in *The Book of Her Life*, immediately upon recounting the vision of Christ in the center of the soul and ourselves as a kind of mirror of Christ, Teresa tells us that this vision also gave her a clearer understanding of sin: "I was given an understanding of what it is for a soul to be in mortal sin. It amounts to clouding this mirror with mist and leaving it black; and thus this Lord cannot be revealed or seen, even though He is always present giving us being" (L 40.5). Elsewhere, she says that it was revealed to her that a person in sin is like a person tied and blindfolded who remains in great darkness (ST 20).[2]

    We are a "clouded mirror" of Christ in that our actual lives and actions can mar and even obstruct the divine image that is our truest reality. We are made to love as God loves, but our loving can include so much neediness and even self-serving. We are

---

2. To this horror at the reality of sin, we might add Teresa's vision of hell that she recounts in the thirty-second chapter of *The Book of Her Life* in which God revealed to her "the place the devils had prepared there for me and which I merited because of my sins."

made for communion with God and with others, but we can too easily find ourselves alienated from one or the other, or both. We are made to live in the full liberty of the children of God—truly free to give ourselves to God without reserve in return for the divine self-gift—but we can so readily squander our freedom on what is infinitely less than God or allow our liberty to become enslaved by lesser things. Rather than reflecting God in our lives as spotless mirrors, we can obscure the divine presence and invitation to others and become blind to it ourselves.

For Teresa, sin does not eliminate the soul's fundamental beauty, nor does God cease to dwell at the inmost center of the soul. Our creation in the image of God is permanent, as is God's abiding presence within us. The tragedy of mortal sin, Teresa tells us, is that although God continues to dwell and shine brightly within the center of the soul, the person is cut off, separated from God and from his or her own truest center. The person in mortal sin is blinded to the divine light from within and thus lives in a terrible darkness. It is as if, Teresa says, one were to place a black cloth over a crystal that sits in the sun and has the potential to reflect it brilliantly, but in sin, the beautiful crystal that is the soul is unable to reflect the divine (IC 1.2.3). God continues to hold sinners in existence, grounding their very being at every moment, but they have alienated themselves from God, from the source of good in their life and from the only path to finding their truest identity. Sin then is fundamentally a self-contradiction—acting against who and what we are and are meant to be.

We can find again a parallel to early Christian thought. Many of the church fathers spoke of both our image and our likeness of God, reflecting the presence of both terms in the Genesis creation text (Gn 1:26). Even after sin, the image of God remains in every human person, but the likeness to God is lost. Sin makes us lose our resemblance to God. The task, according to the church fathers, is to restore the likeness to God through overcoming our sin. We must be transformed once again into what we are: God's own image.

Just so, for Teresa, the task of the person in the outermost dwellings is to overcome the reality of sin in his or her life, progressively at an ever deeper level. The ascetical or liberating part of the inner journey can be seen as the advancing effort, with the help of God, to uproot sin at its depths through a deepening critical self-knowledge, humility, detachment, and generous self-giving. Even in the later dwellings, Teresa tells her readers that they must remain vigilant against the power of sin and its remaining tendencies within.[3]

Teresa urges us not to be halfhearted in our struggle against sin. We must root out not only mortal sin but venial sin as well. Nonetheless, the need to confront our sin does not mean that sin should become our primary focus. We must not allow the recognition of our sin to make us timid in taking up the transforming path, nor tempt us to wallow in a false humility. Teresa knows well from her encounters and union with God that the divine mercy is always greater than our sin. In fact, in *The Book of Her Life*, where Teresa complains that her confessor will not

---

3. Speaking of Teresa's awareness of sin even in the sixth dwelling places, Kieran Kavanaugh makes the fascinating suggestion that at the inner depths attained in these dwellings people become acutely and painfully aware of their own connection and solidarity with the broader human reality of sin. This is the "sin of the world," our unavoidable entanglement with the human history of sin and its continuing legacy and power. Entering into a deeper and more sustained union with Christ who embraced the weight of this burden of sin in his incarnation and redemptive action, people of deep prayer come to share the weight with Christ in a new and different way. Moreover, as people grow closer to the God who grounds our individual and common human existence, they are awakened with growing love for all of those men and women with whom they are embraced by the same God. These people come to a deep awareness of the tragic and ugly reality of our connection in the reality of sin. Coming to share ever more deeply in our redemption in Christ, we cannot avoid a more profound encounter with the sin that, though conquered by Christ, continues to exercise its tragic power in the human condition. Kieran Kavanaugh and Carol Lisi, *The Interior Castle*, study ed. (Washington, D.C.: ICS Publications, 2010), 323.

allow her to go into greater detail about how "wretched" she is, she is really using her sin to highlight God's mercy. In Spanish, she is making a play on words, holding together her *miserias* (that is, her miserable state, her sin) and the *misericordias* (mercies) of God. For Teresa, sin and vice must be honestly acknowledged and overcome with God's help, but we must keep moving. We must remain resolute on the journey toward the center of the interior castle, passing from room to room, dwelling to dwelling, pursuing at the same time the deepening self-knowledge that sees both ourselves as we truly are and God in the divine reality (IC 1.2.8–9). In this way, Teresa holds together both the sense of the greatness of human dignity and a profound sense of the reality and lingering power of sin.[4]

Teresa's attention to sin may require some further comment in our contemporary religious culture. We live in a world today in which there is a profound loss of a sense of sin. Many sincere Catholics no longer celebrate the sacrament of reconciliation because they are not sure that they are guilty of sin. They are aware that they "make mistakes." They know they aren't perfect. But sin? Perhaps it is true that before the Second Vatican Council, there was an overemphasis on sin and a tendency to see God as the heavenly judge who keeps a record of every possible sin, great and small. But now the danger is that there is little attention to sin, little understanding of sin, and little challenge to overcome it. How can you confront an enemy that you don't see or perhaps you aren't even sure exists? The loss of a sense of sin cuts to the core of our Christian faith. As I say, "No sin, no savior." If we aren't sinners, we don't need a savior. If we don't think we are sinners, then why do we personally need a savior? For many, God seems to have been transformed from a stern judge to a permissive

---

4. Alvarez, *Comentarios*, 574.

and doting grandfather. The perfectly appropriate contemporary emphasis on God's love and the divine mercy that is greater than sin has sometimes made us neglect the experience and insight of those like Teresa (and of our Christian tradition) who have no doubt that we cannot be fertile ground for contemplation unless and until we have confronted directly the reality of our sin.

We can certainly read Teresa's horror at the reality of sin as part of her particular religious culture. We can read her own regular assurances that she herself was such a great sinner as the result of her closeness to God. Just as an object's flaws become clearer as it comes closer to a light, so too as saints draw near God, they see the reality and the roots of their sin more clearly. And so they typically describe themselves as "the greatest sinner of all." But even placing Teresa's teaching on sin in its proper context does not negate the presupposition that is central to her teaching and to our spiritual tradition: the transformation that prepares us for communion with God includes recognizing sin, admitting that we are sinners, repenting of our sin, and with God's help overcoming it in our actions and in its roots deep within us.

THE ENTRANCE IS PRAYER AND SELF-KNOWLEDGE

The doorway to the interior castle, says Teresa, is prayer and reflection (IC 1.1.7). She will emphasize the importance of self-knowledge throughout the Christian life, as we shall see when we look at her discussion of humility in a forthcoming chapter. But what she urges at the beginning of the journey is not a form of psychological self-reflection. It is rather attention to God, to our truest reality in God, and thus to our interior life. Since we are created in the divine image and God dwells within each of us, it is prayer and a prayerful reflection of who we are in relation to God that will set us on the right course.

The sad reality, says Teresa, is that many people are completely and blithely unaware and even uncaring of the profound truth of the beauty of our soul and the presence of God within each of us. And so, we do not and cannot really know ourselves. Without prayer and prayerful self-reflection, we remain ignorant of who and what we truly are. Wouldn't it be a shame, Teresa asks, if we didn't know ourselves (IC 1.1.2)? Imagine, she continues, if we encountered someone who was completely ignorant of his or her origins, parents, or native country. We would think such a person tremendously stupid! And yet this is the sad description of people who are focused on external, superficial things, not even reflecting on the dignity and beauty of their soul and therefore neglecting to maintain the great beauty that is God's gift to each of us.

> Teresa bemoans the tragic reality that many people live outside their own castle altogether. They live with their entire focus on superficial things outside themselves, as if those things were the whole of reality.

LIVING OUTSIDE ONE'S OWN CASTLE

Before guiding her readers into the first and outermost dwellings of this interior castle, Teresa bemoans the tragic reality that many people live outside their own castle altogether. They live with their entire focus on superficial things outside themselves, as if those things were the whole of reality. They are immersed in what she calls "foul-smelling worms" and insects that seem to them to be treasures worth pursuing. Her point is not that the world or created things are evil in themselves. Not at all. Teresa of Avila is no dualist. Rather, she is saying that our tendency to focus on such things and ultimately to become blinded and enslaved by them prevents us from looking within to see a far greater beauty and value. People who allow themselves to be immersed and enslaved by what are ultimately trivialities close themselves to the stirrings and invitation of God to begin the journey to discover the divine life within them and thus their truest reality (IC 1.1.3, 5).

Life outside one's own castle is a life without God, without authentic self-reflection, wasting oneself in superficialities. It is the tragedy of people who lose their true, interior identity and instead pour themselves out in the exterior, building a misshapen identity.[5] From neglect of God and the beauty of the soul within and from constant attention instead on the vermin that count as treasure in that purely exterior world, people can make themselves "like brute beasts" (*en semejante bestialidad*; IC 1.1.7; also 1.1.6). As she will say a little further in the *Interior Castle*, "Well now, it is foolish to think that we will enter heaven without entering into ourselves, coming to know ourselves, reflecting on our misery and what we owe God, and begging Him often for mercy" (IC 2.1.11).

Teresa's lament could not be more timely. So much in contemporary society encourages us to live at the level of the passing and even the trivial. Advertising urges us to get the latest, the fastest, and the glitziest. Moreover, life can be so busy—with work or family obligations, whether one is employed or even retired—that there seems precious little time to think, to look

---

5. Ibid., 557.

at our lives, or to pray. When we do have free time, there is easy and often mindless entertainment so readily available, whether through hundreds of cable and satellite television channels or through the Internet. People can spend endless hours on their mobile devices messaging, checking their feeds, playing games, or surfing the Internet. Often enough it doesn't even occur to us that we might just stop and do nothing—nothing except think, or pray, or simply "be."

But the temptation to live at the level of the passing and trivial is not simply a matter of distraction and seemingly relentless activity. The fact is that our society often encourages us to live our lives in search of things such as money, possessions, status, the envy of others, or pleasure. Teresa would address this tendency in her teaching on the three essential virtues. We are tempted to make such things our life's goal or purpose.

A full human life runs deeper than the activities that can fill our days. In short, there is a truer "me" underneath my activity.

Often enough our busyness can be caused precisely by the frenzied pursuit of such transient aims. We can end up living at the level of the superficial because we focus our attention on the trivial and the passing, and we daily interact with people who are doing the very same thing. We become what we seek—become as superficial as the shallow things that we pursue.

Clergy and religious are not necessarily different in this regard—though perhaps in a different form. It is easy enough for us to live lives of endless activity and to seek our own forms of status, the envy of others, and power—just in a different context.

The life of parish priests and other church ministers can be so full of good ministerial activities that we can find it hard to find time to relax, refocus, consider the meaning and value of what we are doing, and pray. And even for those engaged in ministry, a deeper motivation—alongside sincere devotion to one's ministry—can be the desire to be liked, well thought of, and even envied by our peers. And these things are just as shallow as any other transient goals.

Still, there are times that most of us can manage to find an opportunity to ponder our lives. Sometimes, this may occur during vacations or retreats, long drives in a quiet car, or even lying in bed at night. But maybe the challenge and invitation to look more profoundly at our lives comes in a more abrupt or unpleasant way. Illness stops us in our tracks. The realization of death intrudes on our contented or distracted lives. We encounter difficulties, obstacles, and failures that force us to reevaluate. For many of us, it is simply the onset of midlife or the prospect of retirement. We might find ourselves asking about our lives, goals, and accomplishments: "Is that all there is?" What we have been pursuing so actively can look different in the face of death, tragedy, or retirement. "Who am I, really, if I am not all of this activity?" "Who would I be if I didn't have success, money, possessions, status, or power?" "Is there nothing deeper to me or to my life?"

When we take time to ponder, to look at our lives, and take stock, we can begin to see that a truly full life is something deeper and more profound than what we can earn, buy, or possess. We are more than the sum of our activity. A full human life runs deeper than the activities that can fill our days. In short, there is a truer "me" underneath my activity. There is a more authentic life that is not dependent on anything superficial or passing. Beneath my sometimes shallow self that engages in all of this activity or that distracts itself with mindless activity, there is a truer self. Sometimes, if we are lucky and attentive, we can glimpse that inner, more authentic self—a truer life rooted in God—truer than what we often find ourselves actually living from day to day.

Teresa of Jesus invites us to take the step into our own interior castle by prayer and by prayerful self-reflection. She invites us to see ourselves as we are—both full of beauty and dignity as the image of God and in need of ongoing transformation. She challenges us to accept God's invitation to enter into friendship, which is the basis of prayer. And she shows us the way to grow in this friendship, to be transformed so that we can become like our divine friend and thus prepared to receive the divine gift of contemplation and union with God. We now turn to look more closely at her teaching on the transformation that is the necessary preparation for contemplation, and so we turn our principal focus from *The Interior Castle* to *The Way of Perfection*.

3

Prayer and the Three Necessary Virtues

> Before I say anything about interior matters, that is, about prayer, I shall mention some things that are necessary for those who seek to follow the way of prayer; so necessary that even if these persons are not very contemplative, they can be far advanced in the service of the Lord if they possess these things. And if they do not possess them, it is impossible for them to be very contemplative. And if they think that they are, they are being highly deceived. (W 4.3)

*T*he *Way of Perfection,* from which the quotation above is taken, is a book about prayer. In it, responding to the request of her nuns for a teaching on prayer, Teresa offers a kind of handbook, especially on contemplative prayer. But for Teresa and for the spiritual writers of her time, contemplative prayer is a divine gift. With God's help, we can grow in fidelity to and in the depth of our prayer, but contemplation comes only as a gift from God. And as the words above make clear, Teresa believes there is a necessary foundation that we must lay before we can hope to receive this gift. God can, of course, give divine gifts when and to whom God wills, but generally the reception of the gift depends on our preparation. To put it another way, we must prepare the soil so that we can be fertile ground for such prayer.

And this fertile ground is prepared by faithful growth in what Teresa considers three essential virtues that she highlights from the Carmelite constitutions that she wrote for her nuns: "The first of these is love for one another; the second is detachment from all created things; the third is humility, which, even though I speak of it last, is the main practice and embraces all the others" (W 4.4).

The three essential virtues prepare the necessary ground for the gift of contemplative prayer. In order to appreciate why and how this is so, it is important to understand Teresa's basic teaching on prayer, particularly the movement from prayer that is mostly the result of our graced efforts to the contemplative prayer that is essentially a divine gift. It will be useful then to say a few words about the vocabulary that Teresa used to speak of different forms or stages of prayer. Having done so, we will be able to see the foundational role of these virtues, working together, in the transition from "active" to a more "receptive" (that is, contemplative) prayer. Ultimately, for Teresa, prayer and transformation go hand in hand. In order to understand one, we must understand the other. And in order to accomplish one, we must accomplish the other—or God must accomplish it in us.

THE LANGUAGE OF PRAYER

As Teresa begins her explicit teaching on prayer in the second half of *The Way of Perfection*, she begins by explaining different stages of prayer, leading up to contemplative prayer. At its most fundamental level, the spiritual journey begins with vocal prayer. It is "vocal" in the sense that it involves saying words (aloud or to one's self) addressed to God. It involves such practices as saying the prayers that we find in a book, repeating prayers such as the prayer before meals by memory, or our own spontaneous prayers of petition or praise to God.

Mental prayer is simply prayer with attention. Teresa in no way denigrates vocal prayer, but it is not really prayer unless it involves attention to the One whom we are addressing. In that sense, in order to be authentic, vocal prayer must at the same time be mental prayer: "I don't know how mental prayer can be separated from vocal prayer if vocal prayer is to be recited well with an understanding of whom we are speaking to. It is even an obligation that we strive to pray with attention" (W 24.6).

It is of mental prayer that Teresa offers her classic definition of prayer: "For mental prayer in my opinion is nothing else than an intimate sharing between friends; it means taking time frequently to be alone with Him who we know loves us" (L 8.5). As the definition suggests, mental prayer encompasses broader and deeper experiences of prayer, notably what Teresa and other writers of her time refer to as meditation. This refers to prayer that involves the active use of the imagination and intellect in prayer. It can usually be called "discursive" meditation in the sense that it involves moving from one point to another in our prayerful reflection or imagining. Teresa and her contemporary, Ignatius of Loyola, for example, would have been familiar with many books of meditation that offered descriptions of scenes of the life of Christ together with points for prayerful pondering or imagining oneself present in the scene.

It is the purpose of meditation to draw one into the intimate sharing between friends, that is, not to "think much but to love much" (IC 4.1.7; see also F 5.2). Teresa's definition highlights the relational aspect of prayer and its place within a more fundamental relationship or friendship with Christ. Meditation then is meant to lead one into a more affective state of prayer, a deeper personal engagement with Christ. In fact, she tells us that "prayer is an exercise in love" (L 7.12). This is not to say, though, that meditation will always and necessarily bring about the felt presence of God, that is, "consolations" in prayer. Teresa is quite aware of the reality of dryness in prayer and of the necessity to remain faithful to such prayer regardless of what we seem to be experiencing.

For Teresa, meditation is a type of prayer that principally involves our own effort, aided by grace. In our day, the word meditation might be used interchangeably with the word contemplation, or at least the distinction between them might be seen as hazy. But for her, contemplation refers to a type of prayer that can only come as a gift from God. At its heart, it is a wordless awareness or a consciousness of the presence of Christ and of our presence to him that is given to us by God. It does not involve the use of the intellect or the imagination (though they might remain active, in a sense, on their own). We cannot simply choose to engage in contemplation. We can and should strive to prepare for it with a discipline of prayer and with a way of living that it is in conformity with God's will, but God must choose to give it to us, when and as God wills.

In our experience of prayer, the bridge or passage between meditation and contemplation is what Teresa calls recollection. Recollection is simply, as the word suggests, a re-collecting or gathering in of the faculties (intellect, will, and memory/imagination) to become focused or centered in prayer (W 28.4). It must be noted that Teresa is not entirely consistent in her use of the term.[1] In fact, Teresa speaks of both a type of recollection that can be called acquired (that we can bring about) and

---

1. Kieran Kavanaugh and Carol Lisi, *The Interior Castle*, study ed. (Washington, D.C.: ICS Publications, 2010), 138n173. See also Teresa of Avila, *The Collected Works of St. Teresa of Avila*, trans. Kieran Kavanaugh and Otilio Rodriguez (Washington, D.C.: ICS Publications, 1980), 2:489n1. The term "recollection" (*recogimiento*) was very much in use in the spirituality of sixteenth-century Spain, as a spiritual movement for a deeper, quieter form of prayer, led especially by Franciscan reformers and teachers. Teresa herself discovered this prayer of recollection early in her religious life through the book *The Third Spiritual Alphabet* by the Franciscan Francisco de Osuna, given to her by her devout uncle Pedro (L 4.7). This helped her to understand her own experience up to that moment and helped to lay out the spiritual path ahead. She embraced this form

another that is infused (given by God and the entry to true contemplative prayer).

In thinking about acquired recollection, perhaps we might think of contemporary forms of centering prayer in which the person slowly and silently repeats a prayer word or phrase to promote and maintain an inner quiet and attentiveness.[2] Teresa herself does not, strictly speaking, have a "method" of acquired recollection, but she devotes the most focused attention to this form of prayer in chapters 26 through 29 of *The Way of Perfection*.[3] She invites us: "Represent the Lord Himself as close to you and behold how lovingly and humbly He is teaching you. Believe me, you should remain with so good a friend as long as you can" (W 26.1; see also L 9.4). She wants us just to look at Christ who is always present to us and gazing on us with love: "Well now, daughters, your Spouse never takes His eyes off you. He has suffered your committing a thousand ugly offenses and abominations against Him, and this suffering wasn't enough for Him to cease looking at you. Is it too much to ask you to turn your eyes from these exterior things in order to look at Him sometimes?" (W 26.3).

---

or spirit of prayer, though she recounts that her practice of it was not entirely consistent in the years that immediately followed. A careful, thorough examination of the spiritual movements of Teresa's time is provided by Eulogio Pacho, *El Apogeo de la mística cristiana: Historia de la espiritualidad clásica española, 1450–1650* (Burgos, Spain: Editorial Monte Carmelo, 2008). For the discussion of this spiritual movement and of the central meaning of "recollection," see especially the lengthy chapter 5, pages 393–613.

2. Ernest E. Larkin, "The Carmelite Tradition and Centering Prayer/Christian Meditation," in *Carmelite Prayer: A Tradition for the 21st Century*, ed. Keith J. Egan, 202–22 (New York: Paulist Press, 2003). See also, Ernest E. Larkin, "Teresa of Avila and Centering Prayer, St.," in *Carmelite Studies*, vol. 3: *Centenary of Saint Teresa*, ed. John Sullivan, 191–211 (Washington, D.C.: ICS Publications, 1984), available at Carmel Net, http://www.carmelnet.org/larkin/larkin.html.

3. ICS Publications has prepared an excellent pamphlet that describes this type of acquired recollection—the closest to what we might call Teresa's "method": *The Prayer of Recollection* (Washington, D.C.: ICS Publications, 2012). See also Teresa of Avila, *The Way of Perfection*, study ed., prepared by Kieran Kavanaugh, trans. Kieran Kavanaugh and Otilio Rodriguez (Washington, D.C.: ICS Publications, 2000), 23–25.

Note that, in inviting us to "represent" Christ as close to us, Teresa is not really asking us to imagine Christ as such. Rather, she is inviting us to become aware or conscious of his presence in an attentive way. For Teresa, this is not discursive meditation. It is not an active thinking about or imagining of Christ: "I am not asking you now that you think about Him or that you draw out a lot of concepts or make long and subtle reflections with your intellect. I'm not asking you to do anything more than look at Him" (W 26.3).

Just as in centering prayer, in which one uses a word or phrase to focus or to refocus one's recollection, Teresa does invite us to represent Christ in different moments of his earthly life as these might be helpful to us: "If you are joyful look at Him as risen. . . . If you are experiencing trials or are sad, behold Him on the way to the garden . . . or behold Him bound to the column . . . or behold Him burdened with the cross" (W 26.4–5). It is important to see, though, that Teresa is inviting us simply to "behold" Christ in these moments. She is not at this point inviting us to enter into an imaginative reflection on the scene. Rather, she is proposing that we use this representation of Christ—whether a mental picture or an actual painting—as a tool to remaining focused, attentive, recollected.

In our contemporary way of speaking about prayer, we might call such a practice "contemplative," but for Teresa, this is not yet the case. The activity of bringing about recollection through choosing to become prayerfully focused on Christ is still principally our work. It sets the necessary stage for the divine gift of contemplation, but it is not yet there. In *The Interior Castle*, Teresa tells us that the true beginnings of gifted, contemplative prayer occur in the fourth dwellings, and it is introduced by God as infused recollection. Again, this involves a kind of gathering in or re-collecting of the faculties—but now by God's action and thus a deeper experience of the divine presence (IC 4.3).

To distinguish between active prayer and truly contemplative prayer, Teresa uses the image of two founts of water, each with its trough from which to drink: one is fed by many aqueducts from far away and the other by a spring that wells up within its trough, filling it, and overflowing. The first fount is active prayer; the second is contemplation (IC 4.2.2–4).

The Interior Castle then unfolds the further flowering of contemplative prayer: from infused recollection into the prayer of quiet and then into deeper experiences of union with God leading up to an abiding union with God that Teresa calls spiritual marriage.

PERSONAL TRANSFORMATION AND PRAYER

What is absolutely essential to note is that Teresa's discussion of acquired recollection, beginning in chapter 26 of *The Way of Perfection*, follows the first half of the book which focuses on the necessary virtues, that is, the essential transformation of life that must accompany growth in prayer and lays the necessary groundwork for contemplative prayer. In the same way, Teresa's teaching on the beginnings of contemplative prayer in the fourth dwellings of *The Interior Castle* and its unfolding in the remaining three dwellings presupposes the work at prayer and transformation that has occurred in the first three dwellings.

It can be helpful and appropriate to pull out Teresa's teaching on the development and stages of prayer and to summarize them as we have done above. But what can be done for the sake of study and understanding cannot be done in the actual unfolding of prayer in the life of the person who hopes to grow in prayer. For Teresa, it is not enough to know and practice the "method" of acquired recollection. It is not enough to work at the habit and discipline of prayer. The second half of *The Way of Perfection*, which focuses explicitly on prayer, presupposes the book's first half. It is true that Teresa is capable of what seem like long digressions in her writings, but chapters 4 through 18 of *The Way* are no digression. In the same way, the last four dwelling places of *The Interior Castle*, which describe contemplative prayer, can be studied without the first three dwellings, but they cannot be experienced without actually engaging the work of the first three dwellings. Dwellings one through three are not optional, nor are they useful for some people but not others.

As she unfolds her teaching in *The Way of Perfection*, Teresa seems aware that some of her readers will think that her lengthy discussion of virtues is a digression. Nonetheless, she is insistent that the work of the virtues cannot be bypassed:

> You will ask me, daughters, why I am speaking to you about virtues when you have enough books to teach you about them, and you will say that you wanted to hear only about contemplation. I say that had you asked about meditation I could have spoken about it and counseled all to practice it even though they do not possess the virtues, for meditation is the basis for acquiring all the virtues. . . . But contemplation is something else, daughters. . . . Therefore, daughters, if you desire that I tell you about the way that leads to contemplation, you will have to bear with me if I enlarge a little on some other matters even though they may not seem to you so important; for in my opinion they are. And if you don't want to hear about them or put them into practice, stay with your mental prayer for your whole life, for I assure you and all persons who aim after true contemplation . . . that you will not thereby reach it. (W 16.3–5)

Her conclusion is unambiguous: "I say that the King of Glory will not come to your soul—I mean to be united with it—if we do not make the effort to gain the great virtues" (W 16.6).

If our efforts at praying are not accompanied by our efforts at transforming our lives more generally, we simply cannot experience real growth in authentic prayer, and we cannot prepare ourselves for the gift of contemplation. In that sense, any reflection on Teresa's teaching on prayer remains incomplete without her teaching on life transformation. Perhaps many of us would like to read Teresa of Avila on prayer, put its teaching into practice, and find ourselves in contemplative prayer. Certainly, as Teresa notes, God can do what God wants, when God wants, and for whom God wants. But barring a highly unexpected divine intervention, we must engage in the more humble and mundane work of calling upon God to help us transform our lives (W 16.6).

> Any reflection on Teresa's teaching on prayer remains incomplete without her teaching on life transformation.

Obstacles to Prayer and Contemplation

As we know from our own experience, growth in prayer is hard work. For those of us who are beginners in prayer, this is one of the first, most basic, and difficult obstacles to growth in prayer. While there can be moments when we feel God's presence with us, sometimes intensely, and prayer seems effortless, sustained prayer requires discipline and, as Teresa insists, determination. We must work to remain attentive in mental prayer, focused in meditation, and struggling with distractions in acquired recollection. God is with us at every moment, though often it is not apparent to us at all. Teresa recounts her own struggle to remain faithful to her prayer: "And very often, for some years, I was more anxious that the hour I had determined to spend in prayer be over than I was to remain there, and more anxious to listen for the striking of the clock than to attend to other good things. And I don't know what heavy penance could have come to mind that frequently I would not have gladly undertaken rather than recollect myself in the practice of prayer" (L 8.7).

In a later chapter, we will look more closely at Teresa's insistence on persistence and determination in prayer, especially at its beginnings. Without it, we will neither grow in prayer nor be able to be receptive to the contemplative gift.

But difficulties and obstacles in prayer go deeper than a weakness in our resolve or a lack of determination. Drawing closer to God in prayer, entering more deeply into relationship with the divine, requires a broader conformity of our lives with God's will and God's ways. The very fact that Teresa defines prayer in terms of "an intimate sharing between friends" immediately places growth in prayer in the context of a larger growth in the relationship itself. As we have seen, when in the *Life* she defines prayer as this intimate exchange, she follows it immediately by saying, "In order that love be true and the friendship endure, the wills of the friends must be in accord." If the life of the person who seeks to grow in prayer is not in accord with God's will—if he or she does not live in conformity to God's will—"you will endure this pain of spending a long while with one who is so different from you." We cannot enjoy the intimate sharing with God that is prayer, flourish in our friendship with God, or be able to endure time spent with God if we do not conform our ways of being and acting with the divine.

At one level, we can be simply distracted—in this case, not distracted *in* prayer but rather distracted *from* prayer. Teresa describes this reality especially in the second dwelling places of

The Interior Castle in which people desire to grow in prayer but continue to experience the temptation and distraction of what would draw them away from prayer and the journey toward God. In our life in general, we can allow ourselves to be too focused on what is not necessarily bad in itself but which is infinitely less than God and even superficial. Rather than devote ourselves to prayer and to the work of ongoing conversion by which we prepare the soul's soil for contemplation, we focus our attention on lesser things, perhaps some of them not worthy of one created so beautifully in the image of God.

Distraction is one thing. Attachment and enslavement to what is less than God is another, far more deadly to growth in prayer and the personal transformation that is its foundation and fruit. God wants to give the divine life itself to us. At one level, we may sincerely desire to accept this awesome gift and to respond with the gift of ourselves in return. But when we are attached to things that are less than God, both the acceptance and the self-donation are impossible, at least at the profound level to match God's self-offering to us. God invites us into prayer, and with each advance in prayer, we are invited to respond more deeply. But to the degree that our freedom is fixed on what is less than God or merely superficial, we cannot do so.

In our daily lives, we may not feel particularly attached or ensnared, but deeper reflection can reveal its presence in our lives. We are more attached to possessions, to status, to control, to the respect of others than we realize. Sometimes, this recognition of our enslavement is not freely chosen by us. It is, rather, being unwillingly deprived of them that reveals their power over us. We might suffer unexpected financial loss. We could lose some position of power or status, or simply retire from it. Our reputation could be damaged by misunderstanding or malice. Any of these unwanted experiences—and countless others—can reveal a deeper level of neediness and attachment in ourselves than we might previously have realized. Teresa was deeply aware of the reality of this enslavement of our wills—our freedom's ability to respond to the divine self-gift:

> How our will deviates in its inclination from that which is the will of God. He wants us to love the truth; we love the lie. He wants us to desire the eternal; we, here below, lean toward what comes to an end. He wants us to desire sublime and great things; we, here below, desire base and earthly things. He would want us to desire only what is secure; we, here below, love the dubious. Everything is a mockery, my daughters, except beseeching God to free us from these dangers forever and draw us away from every evil. (W 42.4)

A Necessary Path of Liberation

The transformation that is necessary preparation for contemplative prayer is really a liberation of our freedom. Maximiliano Herráiz, a noted Spanish Teresian scholar, describes *The Way of Perfection* as both a catechism on prayer and a tract on freedom.[4] As Teresa herself says of *The Way*, "Hence, do not be surprised, Sisters, about the many things I have written in this book so that you might attain this liberty" (W 19.4). In speaking of *The Interior Castle*, Herráiz proposes that it can be read as a progressive interiorization of freedom. Each of the dwellings of the castle is a deeper stage of freedom as we draw closer to God who dwells within and who is both the font and the goal of all true freedom and liberation.[5]

---

4. Maximiliano Herráiz, *Solo Dios Basta: Claves de la espiritualidad teresiana*, 5th ed. (Madrid: Editorial de Espiritualidad, 2000), 352.

5. Ibid., 368.

Teresa's "asceticism" has nothing to do with a view of the world and its occupations as evil. It is certainly not a misguided effort to move from the bodily to the purely spiritual. It is rather the hard work—which only God can ultimately accomplish in us—of liberating our freedom to accept gratefully and respond completely to God's unmerited self-offering to us.

Teresa refers to this process as the gradual attainment of an authentic "self-dominion," a freedom from enslavements and from the false dominion over us of things such as excessive self-concern, possessions, and worldly honor. It is a kind of mastery over our freedom so that we can truly respond to God—not a freedom that leads to an illusory autonomy from God but a freedom to surrender to God. *The Way of Perfection*, argues Herráiz, can be understood as the description of the path to a progressive self-dominion and thus a deeper freedom.[6]

> Teresa herself tells us that mystical gifts are not essential for the attainment of our freedom. But, as deeper encounters with God, they speed the work of liberation.

This liberating work begins with the help of grace, proceeds with sustained effort over time and with the help of grace received in prayer, and is finally accomplished (as much as is possible in this life) as a fruit of God's presence and action within us. Teresa herself tells us that mystical gifts are not essential for the attainment of our freedom, but as deeper encounters with God, they speed the work of liberation (L 21.8). In fact, with

---

6. Ibid., 374–76.

every infused experience of prayer, Teresa herself felt a greater freedom and self-dominion (L 20.23, 25; L 34.3; ST 2.2).

Teresa is very conscious of the reality of sin. Some people think she is overly conscious of sin, attributing this to the religious culture in which she lived. Regardless, serious sin is always an obstacle to growth in prayer, for how can we grow in prayer if we act in a manner contrary to the will of the One who invites us into prayer and seeks to draw us into closer relationship? But, in relation to her teaching on prayer, Teresa simply presupposes that we must work to overcome sin. The sin that is the focus of her attention—and that must be the focus of attention for those who have overcome serious sin—is not in its form as immoral action or violation of a commandment. Rather it is the enslavement to what is less than God and thus cannot lead us to God or deepen our relationship with the divine friend. Teresa is concerned with the roots of our alienation from God and with what prevents us from deepening the relationship that God is infinitely more anxious to form. Our lack of freedom is a reality to be greatly feared (IC 1.2.11).

It is important to see that, for Teresa, the deepening of prayer is a matter not just of divine presence but of union. God wants to give the divine life to us, fill us with the inflow of the divinity, and ultimately make us one with the divine nature. God wants the friendship that is the foundation of prayer to become the true union of God and the human person. In her writing, Teresa seeks to guide us from the friendship that is the foundation of prayer into the union that is the spiritual marriage—becoming one with God as husband and wife become one flesh. But as God gives the gift of self, so must we. And as God gives totally, so must we. There is no union with God without self-donation.

The deepest prayer and union with God requires the complete gift of ourselves to God, and Teresa knows that she must guide us in the ways of this self-gift if we are to attain the prayer about which she teaches: "Everything I have advised you about in this book," Teresa says in *The Way of Perfection*, "is directed toward the complete gift of ourselves to the Creator, the surrender of our wills to His, and detachment from creatures" (W 32.9). It is only through this self-gift, which is so difficult for us to make, that we can hope to attain prayerful union with God. And so she continues: "Unless we give our wills entirely to the Lord so that in everything pertaining to us He might do what conforms with His will, we will never be allowed to drink from this fount [i.e., " perfect contemplation"]." When it comes to our giving in response to the divine self-offer, there can be no half measures, no partial giving, no holding back: "Whether you have little or much, He wants everything for Himself; and in conformity with what you know you have given, you will receive greater or lesser favors" (IC 5.1.3).

On our own, we are "so miserly and so slow in giving ourselves entirely to God" that we do not fully prepare ourselves to receive what God wants to give (L 11.1). She warns us too of our capacity to be self-deceived about the depth of our giving: "It seems to us that we are giving all to God, whereas the truth of the matter is that we are paying God the rent or giving Him the fruits and keeping for ourselves the ownership and the root" (L 11.2).

Looking at the necessity of this foundation in another way, Teresa also describes this process as a progressive emptying of the self so that God can fill us with the divine life: "The whole point is that we should give ourselves to Him with complete determination, and we should empty the soul in such a way that He can store things there or take them away as though it were His own property. . . . And since He doesn't force our will, He takes what we give Him; but He doesn't give Himself completely until we give ourselves completely" (W 28.12). We are, she is saying, like a container that is already full. We want to fill it with God, and God wants to fill it with the divine life, but the vessel of ourselves is already full with what is less than God. And so, we cannot receive the great treasure that God wants to give. If, Teresa says, we fill the palace of our souls "with lowly people and trifles, how will there be room for the Lord with His court?" (W 28.12). Until we set out on the path of self-emptying, we find that we can receive the gift of the divine self-giving only "drop by drop" when God wants to give it all (L 11.3). The three necessary virtues are instruments to empty ourselves of what is not God, so we can be filled at last with the fullness of the divine life itself.

The Essential Tools for Our Liberation

For Teresa, the three necessary virtues of love of neighbor, detachment, and humility are a kind of three-pronged attack on what is false or superficial within us—those things that are ensnaring our freedom and filling us and thus keeping us from giving ourselves to God as we are being invited. Their aim is a true liberty of spirit grounded in an authentic dominion over ourselves, our desiring, our choosing, our acting, and our loving.

Each virtue is a corrective or an instrument of liberation in the face of distinct forms of enslavement and hindrances to our freedom. Love of neighbor purifies or corrects our relationships *with others*; detachment makes right our relationship *with things* of this world; and humility rectifies our relationship *with ourselves*. Or to look at them from another perspective, our self-seeking and egoism are overcome by growth in love of neighbor; our distraction and enslavement are uprooted by detachment; and our delusions about ourselves and about our true status before God are vanquished by humility.[7] All together, these virtues lead us to a true freedom that allows us to love God and ultimately to love people, things, and self rightly.[8]

In *The Way of Perfection*, Teresa identifies and speaks of the three virtues separately, and yet, more deeply, they are one—distinguishable but not separable: "The first of these is love for one another; the second is detachment from all created things; the third is humility, which, even though I speak of it last, is the main practice and embraces all the others" (W 4.4). Later in the *Way*, she will speak of detachment and humility as "inseparable sisters" that must be found together (W 10.3). In fact, having said so, she sings their praises: "O sovereign virtues, rulers over all creation, emperors of the world, deliverers from all snares and entanglements laid by the devil, virtues so loved by our teacher Christ who never for a moment was without them! Whoever has them can easily go out and fight with all hell together and against the whole world and all its occasions of sin."

So important, in fact, are the development of these virtues and their transforming work that those who, for whatever reason, do not become contemplatives should not think themselves on a lower path to God. God leads according to different paths. Being a contemplative is not necessary for salvation (W 17.2). Teresa cautions that those who have received contemplative gifts ought not to be considered better than others. Rather, "one should consider the virtues and who it is who serves our Lord with greater mortification, humility, and purity of conscience;

---

7. Ibid., 13.

8. Tomás Alvarez, *Comentarios a las obras de Santa Teresa: Libro de la vida, Camino de perfección, Castillo interior* (Burgos, Spain: Editorial Monte Carmelo, 2005), 303. See also Antonio Mas Arrondo, *Acercar el cielo: Itinerario espiritual con Teresa de Jesús* (Santander, Spain: Editorial Sal Terrae, 2004), 82; and Teresa of Avila, *Way of Perfection*, 20.

this is the one who will be the holiest" (IC 6.8.10). Our authentic fulfillment before God comes with conformity to the divine will, not in any particular experiences or stages of prayer: "The highest perfection obviously does not consist in interior delights or in great raptures or in visions or in the spirit of prophecy but in having our will so much in conformity with God's will that there is nothing we know He wills that we do not want with all our desire, and in accepting the bitter as happily as we do the delightful when we know that His Majesty desires it" (F 5.10). In *The Interior Castle*, she tells us unequivocally that our "perfection" lies in perfect conformity to God's will: "Don't think that in what concerns perfection there is some mystery or things unknown or still to be understood, for in perfect conformity to God's will lies all our good" (IC 2.1.8). In the end, those who remain faithful to this transformative path "will be very much the equals of those who receive many delights" (W 17.3). Teresa reassures her readers that St. Martha, who in the Gospel, along with her sister Mary, welcomed Jesus into their home, was not a contemplative. But she is still a saint now dwelling in heaven (W 17.5).

God Makes It Possible

If we hope to deepen our prayer as an expression of our friendship with God, we must work, with God's help, to lay the necessary foundation. Growth in virtue is a task that takes time. We cannot overnight overcome our selfishness, grow in generous service of neighbor, free ourselves of our attachment to things, and develop the self-critical gaze to see ourselves as we are. This is a process that John of the Cross describes both as an "ascent" up a mountain and as a painful, dark night. But for Teresa and for John, our human effort is neither the first word nor the last. God offers friendship with us, and ultimately God gives the gift of contemplative prayer and divine union. And God guides and empowers us along the way.

God's love for us beckons us, and it will be our love for God that moves and sustains us along the way. In speaking of our love for God, Teresa reminds us that "love begets love" (L 22.14). If we can keep God's love before our eyes, we will awaken and nurture love for God within ourselves in return. The renunciations—the giving up, stripping away—that the foundation of prayer requires must be based on a prior possession. We can let go of what we have to the degree that we can recall what we possess and what God wants to give us. It is the sure knowledge in faith of God's self-giving to us that can empower the hard work of laying the necessary foundation. The virtues are instruments of a love that is begotten from faith in God's love for us. Sadly, for us, we discover that our self-giving can be slow and grudging and thus sometimes quite difficult, but Teresa offers herself as positive proof that our loving God is willing to patiently wait. We can be utterly confident that we will receive constant divine help along the way (L Prol 2; L 8.8; IC 2.1.3).

> Our authentic fulfillment before God comes with conformity to the divine will, not in any particular experiences or stages of prayer.

Love is the foundation of the three virtues, and God is ultimately the source of their growth. Grace is available at every moment. As prayer deepens, we find that God is increasingly the source of our authentic self-dominion. In describing the more advanced experiences of prayer in *The Book of Her Life*, Teresa notes how the experience of union brings "such freedom and dominion over all things that it doesn't know itself" (L 20.23). Deep prayer brings the liberty and self-dominion that is the goal of the virtues of love of neighbor, detachment, and humility. In advanced prayer, the person will be able to exclaim with Teresa, "How great is the dominion of that soul brought here by the Lord; it beholds everything without being ensnared!" (L 20.25). A person brought to that stage, she says, finds a powerful new desire to reach out to others (L 20.25), deeper disdain for its former pride (L 20.26), and reason to laugh over its former acquisitiveness (L 20.27).

Gift and Task

The three virtues then can be described as both a task and a gift. They are the liberating path through which, with God's constant help, we overthrow our various entanglements with what is less than God. As the virtues increase in us, we grow in the true self-dominion and freedom by which we can truly love God. And truly loving God, we can love others and value the things of this world rightly. At the same time, it is God who initiates and sustains us in this process. And as our openness to the working of God grows greater through deepening prayer and greater conformity of our lives to the divine will, it is God who makes these virtues grow and bear fruit in liberty.

4

⁛

LOVE FOR OTHERS

In *The Way of Perfection*, Teresa begins her teaching on the essential virtues with a discussion of the virtue of love for others. If we hope to be fertile ground for contemplative prayer, then we must live out, in a daily and practical way, self-giving love for those around us. If we want to conform ourselves more closely to God through prayer, then we must also conform ourselves to the divine self-giving love in our daily actions. If we desire to make a true and complete donation of ourselves to God in response to the divine self-offer in order to enter into union with the God of love, then we must liberate ourselves of the selfishness that impedes our self-donation to God. It is precisely the daily effort to love the people whom God sends into our lives each day—unselfishly and in deed—that liberates our freedom to love and to give ourselves to God completely as divine union requires.

In the present chapter, as in the early chapters of *The Way of Perfection*, our focus is on love as the transformative agent that frees us to love God and so to receive the divine gift of contemplation and union. At the same time, Teresa is also insistent, as we will see later in this chapter and in a later chapter, that growth in love is necessarily a fruit of prayer. We can only grow in love of others as a fruit of our prayerful communion with the God of love. The deeper our encounter with God, the greater our capacity to love others. Ultimately, authentic union with the God of love must necessarily bear fruit in love of others as God loves them. Teresa herself knew this from experience, and all of her writings on the meaning and practice of love come to us as a fruit of her own already advanced prayer.

Teresa's insistence on the utter necessity of practical love for others in *The Way of Perfection* and in her other writings gives clear testimony that her spiritual vision is not disembodied, excessively otherworldly or inner focused, or separated from the practical realities of daily living and relationships. Teresa is a teacher of the most sublime prayer, but her feet are firmly planted on the ground. For her, prayer cannot be separated from the down-to-earth demands of loving any more than the love of God can be separated from love of neighbor expressed in action.[1]

Teresa was a woman with a tremendous capacity for love and friendship. Later in life, she would look back on a certain neediness or selfishness in her loving and especially in her desire to be loved, but her entire life was characterized by strong and varied relationships. Her letters especially reveal her playfulness, her concern, her affection, and sometimes her sternness with friends. Even great mystics can be loving friends. In fact, they can be truer and more selfless friends, as Teresa's teaching on love will make clear.

In Teresa's plan for the Carmelite reform, each Carmel was to be small—no more than thirteen members (like Christ and the twelve apostles), though she later allowed for a few more members. One of her reasons for insisting on small communities

---

1. Secundino Castro, *Ser Cristiano según Santa Teresa: Teología y espiritualidad*, 2nd ed. (Madrid: Editorial de Espiritualidad, 1985), 350. Maximiliano Herráiz has a particularly good summary of Teresa's teaching on love in the sixth chapter of his *Solo Dios Basta: Claves de la espiritualidad teresiana*, 5th ed. (Madrid: Editorial de Espiritualidad, 2000), 268–350.

was precisely to promote and to ensure the quality of relationships among the nuns. Among them, "all must be friends, all must be loved, all must be held dear, all must be helped" (W 4.7). Their life together must be characterized by loving service to one another. She teaches early in *The Interior Castle* that perfect love of God and neighbor would be the perfection of their life together: "Let us understand, my daughters, that true perfection consists in love of God and neighbor; the more perfectly we keep these two commandments the more perfect we will be. All that is in our rule and constitutions serves for nothing else than to be a means toward keeping these commandments with greater perfection" (IC 1.2.17). She reiterates this point when describing the fifth dwelling places: "Here in our religious life the Lord asks of us only two things: love of His Majesty and love of our neighbor. These are what we must work for. By observing them with perfection, we do His will and so will be united with Him" (IC 5.3.7). In the end, even as Jesus taught in the twofold commandment of love, everything can ultimately be reduced to love: "If we practice love of neighbor with great perfection, we will have done everything" (IC 5.3.9). This is an interesting claim for a great teacher of mystical prayer. It means that the love of God expressed in deep prayer and divine union are inseparably and intimately linked with a practical love of ordinary people. Teresa's spiritual teaching cannot be understood simply as a teaching on prayer, no matter how profound, nor apart from her teaching on the deeper transformation of life that must accompany growth in prayer.

FOUR REASONS TO LOVE

One Teresian scholar has argued that in the course of her writings, Teresa lays out four interrelated and overlapping reasons why we must love.[2] We might say that the first is practical, the second is corroborative, the third is imitative, and the fourth is liberating.

First of all, the great founder and reformer of religious life teaches that love is essential to real community living. "Mutual love," she says, "is so important that I would never want it to be forgotten" (IC 1.2.18). Perhaps this is most obviously true for a very small group of people living an entirely enclosed life. In that context, the possibility of grating on each other's nerves must be particularly great. Fundamentally, though, love for one another is essential to every Christian community and family. Explaining the practical necessity for such love, Teresa begins her teaching by saying that "there is nothing annoying that is not suffered easily by those who love one another—a thing would have to be extremely annoying before causing any displeasure" (W 4.5). And, if offense were to be taken or harm done, mutual love brings with it the quick ability to forgive, even as we have been forgiven by God (W 36.7–8). Such love is an assurance of peace within a community and so within the individual members, and interior peace is a prerequisite for a deepening habit of prayer. In the end, to live in community without love would be to live as "brutes" (W 4.10). As we shall see in the fourth reason, the very effort to live this love in our everyday relationships and encounters is transformative precisely because it is sometimes difficult.

But the reason we must love is far deeper than something merely practical. The second reason that Teresa insists on the need for love of neighbor is that it is commanded by Jesus himself, as is clear from the twofold command to love God and neighbor. We must love others because our Savior demands it.

---

2. Tomás Alvarez, *Comentarios a las obras de Santa Teresa: Libro de la vida, Camino de perfección, Castillo interior* (Burgos, Spain: Editorial Monte Carmelo, 2005), 303.

Moreover, Jesus is the great example of love, especially on the cross (W 33.3; IC 7.4.8). In his teaching and most especially in his suffering and death, Jesus reveals to us that any authentic loving involves self-gift. He is himself the self-gift of God to sinful humanity, and in his humanity, he shows us that love is self-gift to and for others.

Our loving must be an imitation of "the good lover Jesus" (W 7.4) whom Teresa also calls our "commander-in-chief of love" (*el capitán del amor*; W 6.9). Since Christ showed his love for those around us by shedding his blood for them, we cannot refuse to love those for whom he died. Echoing the teaching of 1 John 4:19–21, Teresa teaches that failure to love a neighbor is, at the same time, a failure to love Christ (S 2.2). This is not simply a matter of obedience to a command or of simple imitation. If we hope to grow in a deeper relationship of prayer with Christ, we must be conformed to his example of selfless loving. If we desire to enter into union with him, we must learn to become like him.

The third reason love is essential is that it is the only reliable measure or proof of authentic prayer. The depth or authenticity of prayer cannot be measured by how it feels. The presence of consolations—good feelings in prayer—does not necessarily indicate any real depth of encounter with God. In the same way, the experience of dryness in prayer does not mean that one's prayer is not authentic and even deep. Teresa teaches, "When you see yourselves lacking in this love [of neighbor], even though you have devotion and gratifying experiences that make you think that you have reached this stage [the fifth dwellings of the interior castle], and you experience some little suspension in the prayer of quiet (for to some it then appears that everything has been accomplished), believe me you have not reached union. And beg our Lord to give you this perfect love of neighbor" (IC 5.3.12).

Passionate feelings of love for God do not actually translate into a true love of God any more than the presence of intense emotions, without concrete actions, indicates true love for another person. Genuinely lived love of neighbor is a window into the reality of one's more hidden love for God: "We cannot know whether or not we love God, although there are strong indications for recognizing that we do love Him; but we can know whether we love our neighbor. And be certain that the more advanced you see you are in love for your neighbor the more advanced you will be in the love of God." In fact, she continues, love of neighbor will yield a yet deeper love for God: "For the love His Majesty has for us is so great that to repay us for our love of neighbor He will in a thousand ways increase the love we have for Him" (IC 5.3.8).

Teresa's fourth reason to grow in the essential virtue of love of others is the most central in the preparation for contemplative prayer: growth in selfless love of neighbor is the foundation of the deep interior freedom that makes possible the complete gift of one's self to God. The other three reasons to love converge in this one. As we have seen, love is necessary for community life and the peace that is the essential atmosphere for prayer. But for the individual members of that community (whether it is a religious community, the community of marriage and family, or others), the challenge of learning to love other sinners unselfishly in community is the training ground for love and an instrument of making ourselves more selfless in our self-giving. To follow the command of Jesus to love and to imitate his self-giving on the cross necessarily means to lay down one's life for others. And such love lived out in selfless action is both the fruit and proof of authentic prayer and its foundation.

The transformative aspect of love of others is rooted precisely in the fact that it is sometimes so difficult to do in action. Those we are called to love are sinners, and so are we. Fellow sinners can be difficult to serve, to help, to forgive, and to offer kindness because their sin makes them at times unpleasant, ungrateful, and uncooperative. But the deeper problem is the fact that we ourselves are sinners. We may desire to follow the example of God, as manifest most perfectly in Jesus, to love our enemies, to reach out to sinners, and to forgive. But our sinfulness gets in the way, because it tends to focus our attention all

> The transformative aspect of love of others is rooted precisely in the fact that it is sometimes so difficult to do in action.

too easily on ourselves—on our needs and on our own convenience, desires, and preferences. In our fallen state, we can easily fall into an egocentrism in which we seek and protect our own selfish needs. But true love, after the model of Jesus, is the very opposite of self-seeking. As Teresa writes, reflecting the message of the Gospel, those who love authentically "are more inclined to give than to receive" (W 6.7). For this very reason, the sometimes challenging effort to love others in generous, selfless service can be a real struggle. Overcoming our inherent strain of selfishness can take discipline over time—sometimes seemingly practiced by sheer force of will one day after another, toward one sinful human being after another.

Teresa makes clear that our effort to love even in the face of our selfish reluctance is and must be aided by the grace of God:

> And beg our Lord to give you this perfect love of neighbor. Let His Majesty have a free hand, for He will give you more than you know how to desire because you are striving and

making every effort to do what you can about this love, and force your will to do the will of your Sisters in everything even though you lose your rights; forget your own good for their sakes no matter how much resistance your nature puts up; and, when the occasion arises, strive to accept work yourself so as to relieve your neighbor of it. (IC 5.3.12)

STRIVING FOR FREEDOM TO LOVE

The effort to truly love other people in practice, one day after another, quickly reveals to us that we are not really free to love others as we want or know that we should. Our freedom to love is constrained by the pull and drag of our own tendency to self-centeredness. This is true of our love for both God and neighbor. The essential virtue of love of others—lived out in concrete action, by the sheer force of our will if necessary—is a critical instrument for arriving at the freedom that allows us to receive God's self-giving and to make our own self-donation. We become free to love by choosing to love, one action of service and kindness after another.

Teresa is offering a profound underlying truth about all loving, in every Christian vocation. Like Teresa, St. Benedict taught his monks that they must learn to bear the burdens of the other monks; that is, they must learn to help carry the burdens of the others, and they must also bear the burden that the other monks sometimes are to one another. In the penultimate chapter of his rule for monks, titled "The Good Zeal of Monks," Benedict teaches, "This, then, is the good zeal which monks must foster with fervent love: They should each try to be the first to show respect to the other (Rom 12:10), supporting with the greatest patience one another's weaknesses of body or behavior, and earnestly competing in obedience to one another."[3] Living with the Benedictine vow of stability to the monastery of one's profession, the monk is committing to a lifetime of effort to love, to show patience, and to give mutual obedience within a community of fellow sinners. And the very effort to live and act in this way, one day after another with the same group of flesh-and-blood fellow sinners for a lifetime, is the path to the selflessness by which the monk can truly and freely love God and others. This is the path to the ordinary holiness that is the goal of Benedictine monastic living. It is not just a tool for "oiling the machine" of the common life. Rather, precisely by forbearance, patience, and generous service of others who are sometimes difficult to love (as are we), the monks grow in the self-forgetful love with which Christ loved.

It must be said that there is nothing in Teresa's (or Benedict's) basic teaching about love that is restricted to religious life in community. What she describes is no less the basic dynamic of marital love and parental love. Spouses and parents must strive to love with a greater generosity and genuine other-directedness. Of course, this is not always easy, either in marriage or in family life, as it is not always easy in religious life. But the very effort to grow in such a love brings a greater freedom to love God and others beyond the marriage and family. In his Letter to the Ephesians (5:21–33), St. Paul parallels the love of Christ for his bride the church with the love of a husband for a wife. Christ loves the church precisely in that he lays down his life for her, thus revealing the way that one human spouse should love another. And in marriage, as in religious life, it is the little, daily actions of being attentive, patient, forgiving, and other-directed toward another sinner that empower married people to become freer to love one

---

3. *Rule of Saint Benedict*, chap. 72, in *RB 1980: Rule of St. Benedict in English*, ed. Timothy Fry (Collegeville, Minn.: Liturgical Press, 1982), 94–95.

another and to love God. Self-giving love in simple action is the path to holiness in every vocation.

A CAUTION

Without denying in any way the truth of what has just been said, it is important in our day to offer a caution. Clearly, an exclusive emphasis on self-giving and self-forgetfulness can lead to or support neglect of one's own true worth and even to the acceptance of forms of abuse. A lack of care for one's self cannot be authentic Christian loving. In fact, as the old theological adage says, we must possess something in order to give it away. We must truly possess ourselves in order to give ourselves away.[4] This means practically that we must value ourselves, care for ourselves, and at times stand up for our rights. We ourselves are created in the image of God, and we must respect our own dignity. Allowing others to be abusive or to pursue their unchallenged selfishness is not good for us, nor is it good for them or for other people who might suffer from their egocentric attitudes. Sometimes, we must stand up for ourselves and others. We must take care of ourselves in an authentic way even as we strive to genuinely love others. In this way, we can truly love our neighbor *as ourselves*.

It is true that, in this life, authentic love is self-giving. The cross of Jesus makes this clear, but love at its fullest is something more. Christian love is always seeking to become *mutual* loving. At its fullest, authentic love involves both giving and receiving. We see the mutuality of loving in the life of the Trinity itself. The Persons of the Trinity are eternally self-giving, but theirs is a mutual giving *and* receiving. It is this reciprocal and mutual love

---

4. Teresa cites this adage in another place, though for a different use: "Clearly, no one can give what he does not have; he must have it first" (F 5.13).

that is love's fullest meaning. Even the love of Jesus on the cross was aimed at mutuality; that is, he gave himself in order that we might be able to give ourselves in return. He gave us the model, the invitation, and the empowerment to love God and neighbor in self-giving and as an invitation to love in return. Union with God means receiving the divine gift of self and making the full gift of ourselves in return in mutual loving. The central understanding of love as self-giving must be seen in this broader perspective.

Teresa was acutely aware of the dignity of each person created in the image of God, as she says at the beginning of *The Interior Castle*. Still, there is no doubt that the contemporary world has come to see the value and dignity of the individual person in a way that was not quite so obvious in the sixteenth century. We must read what Teresa says about love, detachment, and humility with contemporary eyes. Still, the truth of what Teresa is saying remains indisputable. Today, we see that

> A lack of care for one's self cannot be authentic Christian loving. In fact, as the old theological adage says, we must possess something in order to give it away.

authentic self-giving must be chosen, and it must be free. We see that we must value and possess ourselves in order to authentically give ourselves away. Nonetheless, even recalling these more contemporary insights, it still remains true that we must give ourselves away in generous and selfless service of others. As long as we remain sinners, we will be plagued with an inherent tendency to be self-serving, with its accompanying lack of freedom to love. And as long as that is the case, then the virtue of practical love of neighbor will remain essential in our lives.

THE TWO KINDS OF LOVE FOR OTHERS

Teresa makes a distinction between two types of love for others (W 4.12).[5] Although she herself found the difference difficult to explain, it offers further help in appreciating practical love as a virtue essential to the reception of contemplative prayer (W 4.11; 6.2).[6] Teresa tells us that the first type of love—and the one most to be pursued—is a spiritual love. Of the second, she says, "The other is spiritual mixed with our sensuality and weakness or good love, for it seems to be licit, as is love for our relatives and friends." We might call this latter, mixed kind of love a merely natural loving. It is not evil. In fact, Teresa says it is good in itself but is easily distorted and can lead to enslavement; it can become an obstacle to a fuller love and to growth in prayer.

For Teresa, the spiritual love that we must seek to nurture with God's help is not some kind of disembodied love. In fact, all true loving involves the entire person. But this is a love that places natural human affections and attractions into the broader context of a desire for the other's true and complete

---

5. Teresa notes that there are also sinful and selfish affections that are sometimes called love but that are in fact not worthy of the name (W 7.2).

6. Kavanaugh notes that she rewrote her discussion on the two types of love more than once. See Teresa of Avila, *The Way of Perfection*, study ed., prepared by Kieran Kavanaugh, trans. Kieran Kavanaugh and Otilio Rodriguez (Washington, D.C.: ICS Publications, 2000), 478–79n8. For my discussion of Teresa's thought on the question, I have been greatly helped by Ernest E. Larkin, "Human Relationships in Saint Teresa of Avila," which originally appeared in *The Land of Carmel: Essays in Honor of Joachim Smet, O.Carm.*, ed. Paul Chandler and Keith J. Egan, 285–97 (Rome: Institutum Carmelitanum, 1991). I accessed it online: Carmel Net, accessed December 17, 2015, http://www.carmelnet.org/larkin/larkin032.pdf, 136–44. See also Rowan Williams, *Teresa of Avila* (New York: Continuum, 1991), 104–10.

good—which for Teresa is communion with God. An authentic spiritual love seeks the whole good of the other—for the sake of the other and not for the sake of the lover. It is "a love with no self-interest at all. All that it desires or wants is to see the other soul rich with heavenly blessings" (W 7.1). Those we truly love are seen with an eye toward eternity and thus with a keener ability to see everything and everyone in their proper context.

It is no wonder then that Teresa argues that it is possible to be at peace with the fact that our loved ones are undergoing trials; that is, if it appears that these struggles are the divine will for them. If they are bearing their difficulties with patience and thus are learning to embrace God's mysterious will for them with humility and trust, then sometimes the best response is to pray that our loved ones will be able to stay the course with faith and perseverance. If the difficulties and struggles of those we love are for their spiritual, holistic good, we cannot wish the situation to be otherwise from them (W 7.3).

Traditionally, what Teresa calls a spiritual love has sometimes been referred to as a "disinterested" love, but the term may be somewhat unfortunate for us today. There cannot really be love without interest for the good of the other. Perhaps we might better speak of love without excessive *self*-interest or of a truly *other*-directed love. It is a love that is uninterested in what is merely *self*-serving but that is keenly interested in the true good of the one who is loved. We must love others, with little care about being loved ourselves (W.6.5–7). Even God, Teresa says, must ultimately be loved without self-interest in the sense that God should be loved for who God is rather than for what God can do for us (IC 4.2.9).

Spiritual love, Teresa insists, it is not a disembodied love, nor is it a love without passion, but its passion is for the other's true good and not for some aspect or attribute that the person possesses or for any benefit to the person who loves. She writes, "It will seem to you that such persons [who love spiritually] do not love or know anyone but God. I say, yes they do love, with a much greater and more genuine love, and with passion, and with a more beneficial love; in short, it is love. . . . I say that this attitude is what merits the name 'love,' for these other base attachments have usurped the name 'love'" (W 6.7). Perfect love is the passion to make the other person truly worthy of love (W 6.9).

Fully authentic love is not some ethereal, utterly transcendent loving. It is lived in small and practical ways, grounded in an attitude that is "more inclined to give than to receive (W 6.7). It is a love with compassion for the weakness and faults of others (W 7.5–6). In communal religious life, it leads the members to engage in recreation with others for their sake and for the sake of the life of the community, even when it runs contrary to a person's preferences at the moment. (The same could said about the active interpersonal engagement of spouses with one another in marriage and of family members in familial life.) This spiritual love overlooks the faults of others, prays for them, and strives to give good example (W 7.7). People who love in this way set aside their own advantage for the sake of others (W 7.8), demonstrated in seeking to relieve the work of others and rejoicing in the virtues of those who are loved (W 7.9). In short, the person who can love in this manner is "imitating that love which the good lover Jesus had for us" (W 7.4). It is a "perfect love" in which "everything is done with a pure intention" (W 7.7).

In response to the possible complaint of her nuns that in their cloister they are not able to do great deeds in God's service, Teresa challenges them to focus on those with whom they live: "In sum, my Sisters, what I conclude with is that we shouldn't build castles in the air. The Lord doesn't look so much at the greatness of our works as at the love with which they are done. . . . Thus even though our works are small they will have the value our love for Him would have merited had they been great" (IC 7.4.15). We must love in practical ways the flesh-and-blood people we find before us rather than regret that we lack opportunities to love in obviously extraordinary and heroic ways or circumstances.

The contrast with merely natural loving ("spiritual mixed with sensuality") helps to make clearer the meaning of fully authentic love. We are naturally inclined to love family, friends, and those who are good to us. We feel a natural attraction and perhaps an easy affection for those who are naturally attractive to us, in whatever way (W 4.7; 6.4). There is nothing wrong with this. Teresa's letters reveal her deep human affection for a large and varied number of family and friends, even after she had arrived at an abiding union with God. Her concern with

> Fully authentic love is not some ethereal, utterly transcendent loving. It is lived in small and practical ways, grounded in an attitude that is "more inclined to give than to receive."

this natural loving is that—without a deeper and broader spiritual vision of ourselves, other people, and the purpose and goal of life—such love can easily become self-focused, distorted, and even enslaving.[7]

---

7. Teresa of Avila, *Way of Perfection*, 72.

Looking at her life, we see that Teresa remained actively engaged throughout her life in loving bonds with her family and friends. But, at the same time, she saw clearly from experience that such bonds can be either part of a holistic relationship with God or a distraction from it. It is easy enough for natural familial and friendly relationships to remain, to veer, or to sink into unhelpful and even harmful directions. At the Monastery of the Incarnation, before her deeper spiritual conversion, Teresa spent a great deal of time visiting with family and old friends in the visiting parlors and even outside, talking about trivialities. Such conversations, as she notes, can easily disintegrate into gossip and worldly topics that offer no real benefit to any party in the conversation. Instead of helping relatives to enter more seriously into the Christian life, the religious merely confirms them in their worldly ways or is herself dragged down by such conversations.

Merely natural loving can easily become excessive. In this regard, Teresa tells us that love can go astray by either defect or excess. It goes awry by defect when people fail to love the people with whom they live and have regular interaction. She says little more of this defect than to say that to live together without love is to live "like brutes" (W 4.10). It is really the other defective way of loving—by excess—that is her focus. The person can become too focused on members of one's family and friends in a manner that does not see them in the larger picture of what is truly good for them or to the exclusion of others. Such love is not really excessive in the sense of loving too much but rather excessive relative to what is really good for the lover and for the person loved. Teresa tells us that it is rarely directed to helping the other person to love God more (W 4.6). And it is distracting to the lover, sapping the strength of will to love God fully (W 4.5). In this sense, this excessive and misdirected loving is an obstacle to the freedom and openness to receive the gift of

contemplation. It is a form of attachment and even an enslavement of our freedom in much the same way that we can be
attached or enslaved by created things.

In *The Way of Perfection*, Teresa takes special aim at what
is traditionally known as "particular friendships." For her, they
are an obvious example of merely natural loving gone awry by a
kind of excess. Such exclusive relationships are harmful to community life and interactions, most especially in a small community, and can become the nucleus of factions and groups in
a community (W 4.5–9). But beyond their impact on communal relations, such friendships inherently include a selfish
focus, a kind of possessiveness that is not about material things
(the focus of the virtue of detachment) but rather a possessiveness about people. Such particular relationships do not lead to
a greater freedom to love generally and broadly. Instead, they
narrow freedom and restrict one's vision. It becomes easy not
to be concerned for the true good of the other—which would
actually be rooted in their participation in wider communal
relations and which is ultimately spiritual and transcendent—
but rather to become too narrowly focused on the other's
immediate comfort or protection (and, at another level, on
one's self).

A quick look at Christian married love shows the truth of
what Teresa is saying. At first glance, it may appear that married
love is always particular in an exclusive way. But this is not the
case. A man and woman brought together in the sacrament of
Christian marriage are not meant to love each other to the exclusion of others. The ideal of Christian marriage as a sacrament
constituted between two Christians is that the spouses love one
another in God. They love God, and they love one another in
God—not more than God, not alongside or in addition to God,
and not to the exclusion of God. Looking again at the Ephesians

marriage text, we see that St. Paul says that Christ showed his love for his bride the church by laying down his life for her, so that he could make her holy. The spiritual, holistic good of the bride is his ultimate concern. If this is so in authentic Christian marriage, then it is also so in genuine Christian friendship. The authentic love of Christian spouses is not exclusive in the sense of closed in on itself. Rather, it is meant to be fruitful beyond the bond between them—children, if God wills it, but also in love for others beyond their marriage and family. And all of this takes work over time aided by grace so that a merely human love and affection between husband and wife can become a more authentically sacramental loving.

For Teresa, natural loving must be taken up into a larger faith vision of who we are—ourselves and those we love—before God. In that larger context, natural bonds are not abandoned but purified and made right. The spiritual love of which Teresa speaks ultimately comes from God as deeper encounters reveal reality in light of what God desires for us and for every other human person. This divine vision and deeper union with the God who is love bears fruit in a manner of loving that is in keeping with who we all truly are before God. Meanwhile, it is a great challenge and task—a task of liberation and transformation—as we work to overcome our self-centeredness, our selfishness, and our distraction by and enslavement to persons and to other things.

LOVE OF GOD, LOVE OF NEIGHBOR

The true flowering of love of neighbor can only ultimately come as the fruit of love of God: "If we practice love of neighbor with great perfection, we will have done everything. I believe that, since our nature is bad, we will not reach perfection in the love of neighbor if that love doesn't rise from the love of God as its root" (IC 5.3.9). As we learn to love God more fully, we will find ourselves able to love our neighbor more generously.

"Prayer," says Teresa, "is an exercise in love" (L 7.12). We pray as an expression of our love for God who has first loved us and called us into friendship. But it is possible that love for God at any particular moment can demand that we attend to the needs of others, even if it draws away from our time of prayer. Such loving service of others, when truly necessary, does not inherently lessen prayer: "And let souls believe me that it is not the length of time spent in prayer that benefits one; when time is spent as well in good works, it is a great help in preparing the soul for the enkindling of love" (F 5.17). Sometimes, God's loving will for us is the active service of neighbor rather than solitude and prayer.[8] Still, Teresa is not recommending activism in place of prayer. She cautions in the same place: "It's necessary to be on one's guard and careful in the performance of good works by having frequent interior recourse to God, even though these works are done in obedience and charity."

As our prayer deepens, we find new impetus to be of service to others. Women and men of advanced prayer "look only at serving and pleasing the Lord. And because they know the love He has for His servants, they like to leave aside their own satisfaction and good so as to please Him and serve. . . . They keep before their minds the benefit of their neighbor, nothing

---

8. St. Vincent de Paul offers the same counsel: "If a needy person requires medicine or other help during prayer time, do whatever has to be done with peace of mind. Offer the deed to God as your prayer. Do not become upset or feel guilty because you interrupted your prayer to serve the poor. God is not neglected if you leave him for such service. One of God's works is merely interrupted so that another can be carried out." This text is quoted in the Office of Readings for the memorial of St. Vincent de Paul on September 27 in *The Liturgy of the* Hours, vol. 4 (New York, N.Y.: Catholic Book Publishing Company, 1975), 1425. Both he and St. Louise de Marillac spoke of this as "leaving God for God."

else. So as to please God more, they forget themselves for their neighbor's sake, and they lose their lives in the challenge, as did many martyrs" (M 7.5).[9]

Active love of neighbor in practical service slowly transforms us, freeing us of any inherent selfishness. In doing so, it enables us to love God more freely. At the same time, love of God is fed in prayer and expressed by prayer. The more we grow in love of God, the more we find reason and empowerment to love the people that God sends into our lives. As we shall see, loving our neighbor freely and generously is finally the fruit of the deepest union with the God who is love.

---

9. Two centuries before Teresa, the great mystic St. Catherine of Siena recounts in her *Dialogue* that God warned her of people who refused to leave their prayer in order to serve others: "These people find all their pleasure in seeking their own spiritual consolation—so much so that often they see their neighbors in spiritual or temporal need and refuse to help them ... But they are deceived by their own spiritual pleasure, and they offend me more by not coming to the help of their neighbor's need than if they had abandoned all their consolations." The text is quoted by Susan Rakoczy, *Great Mystics and Social Justice: Walking on the Two Feet of Love* (New York, N.Y.: Paulist Press, 2006), 34.

5

Detachment

Quien a Dios tiene, nada le falta. Solo Dios basta.

"Whoever has God lacks nothing. God alone is enough." This is Teresa's famous bookmark. It summarizes her teaching on the importance of the virtue of detachment.[1] If we have God, we have everything, both in the sense of having what is of ultimate value and in the sense that in possessing God we are free to possess everything else authentically. For most of us, this profound and fundamental truth is difficult for us to grasp and to attain. In ordinary human living, it is all too easy to be distracted by and attached to things that are infinitely less than God, as though such things could satisfy or fulfill us. We settle for less and thereby make ourselves less than we are meant to be. We need to become detached—free—in order to grasp the communion that God offers and that alone can fulfill us.

Teresa begins her teaching on detachment (*desasimiento*) in chapter 8 of *The Way of Perfection*: "Now let us talk about the detachment we ought to have, for detachment, if it is practiced with perfection, includes everything. I say it includes everything because if we embrace the Creator and care not at all for the whole of creation, His Majesty will infuse the virtues" (W 8.1). We must,

---

1. Félix Málax, "Desasimiento," in *Diccionario de Santa Teresa*, ed. Tomás Alvarez, 2nd ed. (Burgos, Spain: Editorial Monte Carmelo, 2006), 204.

as she says in an emphatic way elsewhere, "abandon completely everything for God" (*dejando todo del todo por Dios*; L 21.12). Such abandonment is precisely what the first disciples did, as the Gospels tell us (Mk 10:28; Lk 5:11). Indeed, it is Jesus himself who, especially on the cross, shows us what true detachment is.

Like the other two necessary virtues—love of others and humility—detachment is a necessary condition for prayer: "I really believe that whoever humbles himself and is detached (I mean in fact because the detachment and humility must not be just in our thoughts—for they often deceive us—but complete) will receive the favor of this water [contemplative prayer] from the Lord and many other favors we don't know how to desire" (IC 4.2.10). At the same time, again like the other two virtues, an increasing detachment is a fruit of deepening prayer (IC 7.3.8).

For Teresa, detachment is nothing else than the necessary condition for truly loving God: "Do you think it is possible for a person who really loves God to love vanities? No, indeed, he cannot; nor can he love riches, or worldly things, or delights, or honors, or strife, or envy" (W 40.3). In this, she is consistent with what Jesus tells us in the Gospel: "No one can serve two masters; for a slave will either hate the one and love the other, or be devoted to the one and despise the other. You cannot serve God and wealth" (Mt 6:24). Teresa is teaching us that the problem is not the world or created goods in themselves but the "vanities" (*vanidades*) of the world. Sometimes when Teresa speaks of these vanities, she means trivial pursuits such as the interest she developed as an adolescent in her appearance and in fine clothes (L 2.2, 3); or her desire as a young nun to appear clever in the monastery's visiting parlor in idle conversation; or her desire to be considered by others as a person of prayer (L 7.1, 13, 14, 17, 18). But the term "vanities" refers more broadly to the normal things of this world whose relative value we distort by allowing ourselves to be distracted by them or attached to them. The good things of this world are vanities in comparison to what God wants to give to us and to be for us (W 28.11). Teresa tells us that the vanities of worldly honor or possessions give a false peace in comparison to the peace that God gives (M 2.10). The things of this world are vanities relative to the authentic "jewels" of divine gifts and favors (L 10.5). She bemoans

> It is precisely Teresa's desire to embrace God and to be embraced by her Beloved that drives her insistence on detachment. Its fundamental purpose is profoundly positive.

parents who are concerned to pass on the vanities of this world (riches and lands) rather than the riches of the faith and of the life to come (F 10.9). And as we have seen, for Teresa, authentic love of God cannot coexist with attachment to such things that are infinitely less than God.

It is precisely Teresa's desire to embrace God and to be embraced by her Beloved that drives her insistence on detachment. Its fundamental purpose is profoundly positive. It is an essential aspect of her choice for God. Otherwise, leaving created things in itself has no particular value. The world is not evil for Teresa. It is just infinitely less than God. And worse, the things of this world can get in the way if we get distracted by or enslaved by them.[2] Detachment promotes the freedom for self-donation to God (W 8.1).

---

2. Maximiliano Herráiz, *Solo Dios Basta: Claves de la espiritualidad teresiana*, 5th ed. (Madrid: Editorial de Espiritualidad, 2000), 124.

In fact, it is detachment from created things that allows us to truly appreciate them in their limited but true beauty and goodness—and not just as things useful for our mundane or even selfish purposes. In God, we come to see and to love them freely and thus authentically: "Those who truly love God, love every good, desire every good, favor every good, praise every good. They always join, favor, and defend good people. They have no love for anything but truth and whatever is worthy of love" (W 40.3). Detachment, she says, changes our taste for the things of this world. It brings us to recognize the bitterness of what this world falsely values and instead to taste the sweetness of what this world disdains. Referring to the Old Testament Book of Exodus (chap. 16; see Wis 16:20–21), she says that the people of Israel couldn't savor the true sweetness of the manna that God provided for them in the wilderness until they gave up their longing for the fleshpots of Egypt (W 10.4).

Before we look more deeply at Teresa's teaching on detachment, it might be useful to note more explicitly the timeliness of her insights for all of us today.

A Teaching for Today

We live in a world of plenty. For most of the readers of this book, we have everything we need and virtually anything that we really want. We have disposable income. We can and do buy far more than we need. In fact, ours is a culture of consumerism and materialism. We are tempted and even actively encouraged by the relentless onslaught of advertising in every possible media to accumulate more and to have more. In this context, it is all too easy to confuse "having" with "being," "having more" with "being more."

"Social sin" is a term that we use to express the way that sin becomes rooted in the structures, relationships, and values of a society. Consumerism and materialism are perfect examples. Personal sin involves our personal engagement, by choice, in evil. The reality of social sin lacks, in itself, the element of choice, but it is built up and maintained by personal choices. It can then have a powerful impact on personal decisions. Today's consumerism is the result of greedy, self-indulgent, superficial choices over time. And we are all impacted and even formed by it. Growing up and living in this culture, we can tend to view reality as well as our own needs and identity through its lenses. We come to believe that we really "need" more, better, more expensive, and yet more up-to-date stuff when, in fact, we do not need more at all. We can come to view ourselves as diminished by having less and as enhanced by having more—even when, in fact, the thing desired is superficial, unimportant, or even harmful.

In our time, as in Teresa's, we can become possessed by our need for possessions. Instead of us truly owning them, they come to own us. We fret about losing what we have, being unable to accumulate more, or being left behind in the dash to have the newest and the best.

Even for those of us who sincerely profess our Christian faith and who desire earnestly to deepen our relationship with God, we feel the tug—if not the pull—of possessions. We are not immune, for example, from the attraction of having the latest gadgets. And having purchased the most up-to-date technology, we enjoy it and explore its potentials—until the next update or version comes along. Simply being Christian is no protection against the lure of a consumerist culture. Unless we allow our faith and the deeper insight that comes from prayer to open our eyes to the true scale of values, we are doomed to live as so many others in our culture—unable to truly savor the divine manna that our God wants to give.

It is certainly a positive characteristic of our contemporary Christian culture that we do not view the material world in itself as evil or suspect. We are not tempted to believe that created things are evil in themselves. But really, neither was Teresa. She didn't have a negative view of the world or a suspicion about the fundamental goodness of creation. It's just that she saw through the glitz, the "bling," of her own day—the "vanities" of this world. She saw that created goods have only relative value and that, in comparison with the possession of God, they have very little value. In fact, she recounts how when her friend and benefactor, Doña Luisa de la Cerda, showed to Teresa her rich jewels of gold and precious stones in order to cheer the saint during an illness, Teresa laughed inwardly at what people of this world esteem so highly (L 38.4). For Teresa, so unimaginably wonderful is the possibility of possessing God and being fully possessed by the divinity that nothing else could possibly measure up. If anything other than God and what leads to divine communion might distract or obstruct us, it simply must be let go of—and the sooner and the more completely, the better.

Teresa's teaching about detachment is in no way some antiquated relic of a bygone spirituality. We haven't grown beyond the need for what she has to say. In fact, we probably need it more in our day than did her original readers. This great spiritual master offers a timeless insight into our sinful human condition. We tend all too easily to desire and grasp after things that are infinitely less than the communion with God that alone can satisfy and fulfill us. And desiring and pursuing these lesser things, we become enslaved by them. We need to be detached from them in order to become truly ourselves and to attain communion with God. Teresa continues to challenge each of us, whatever our circumstances or state in life, to maintain a critical self-examination of our relationship to material goods in light of our faith and the ultimate aspirations of our lives.

DETACHMENT AND FREEDOM

As we found in our discussion of the three essential virtues, the liberating and transformative path of Teresa involves growth in a deeper freedom. Growth in communion with God and openness to receive the gift of contemplation requires our freedom. And the liberty to love and receive fully from God requires detachment from all that is less than God. As we shall see, the issue is not so much about owning or enjoying external things but rather our internal disposition toward things, where we place them in the scale of ultimate values, and our freedom to let them go and walk away from them in order to pursue what is infinitely more valuable and worthy.

The immediate goal of detachment is self-dominion or self-mastery, freedom from enslavement to things other than God. Its final goal is the freedom that allows us to love God completely. We recall again the old and self-evident adage that you have to possess something in order to give it away. Detachment allows us to possess ourselves—instead of being possessed by our possessions—so that we can give ourselves to God in response to the divine self-giving.

In reflecting on her own life, Teresa saw in herself an attachment not so much to things but rather to people—or really, to being loved by others. This attachment, like any other, left her un-free. In *The Book of Her Life*, she describes her struggle to love in a selfless way and simply to receive the love of others without being attached to or enslaved by it. In hindsight, she says that in her youth she felt a strong need to be loved. She found herself attracted to anyone whom she felt loved her (L 37.4). She became enslaved by this neediness. In *The Way of Perfection* too, she tells us that she came to perceive her own efforts to secure and hold onto the love and affection of others. The cause of her concern was obviously neither love nor being loved. The problem was the element of enslavement (W 9.3). And this form of disordered attachment, as any other, crippled her freedom to love others and to love God.

Ultimately, Teresa came fully to freedom from this attachment only as a divine gift when God said to her, "No longer do I want you to converse with men but with angels" (L 24.5). From that point on, she felt a freedom from her attachments (L 24.5–8). She concludes her reflection, "May God be blessed forever because in an instant He gave me the freedom that I with all the efforts of many years could not attain by myself" (L 24.8). For Teresa, mystical graces always bring greater freedom and detachment (e.g., L 34.3; ST 2.2). Detachment brings freedom, and true freedom allows us to love God and neighbor selflessly.

Paradoxically, Teresa sometimes expresses the goal of freedom as exchanging slavery to the world for slavery to Christ: "Let us not condescend, oh daughters, to allow our wills to be slaves to anyone, save to the One who bought it with His blood" (W 4.8). Teresa means by this seemingly odd manner of expression that our freedom is made for God, and giving it completely to God is its very purpose. Teresa's contemporary, St. Ignatius of Loyola, expresses the same sentiment when he famously prayed that the Lord would take all his liberty.

In the seventh and inmost dwelling places of the interior castle, Teresa tells us that the person arrives at true union with God and, at the same time, is directed to the service of others after the model of Jesus. One of the ways that she expresses this truth is again with the image of slavery: "Do you know what it means to be truly spiritual? It means becoming slaves of God. Marked with

His brand, which is that of the cross, spiritual persons, because now they have given Him their liberty, can be sold by Him as slaves of everyone, as He was" (IC 7.4.8). "Sold as slaves of everyone" means a life of loving and humble service for others.

DETACHMENT AND RELIGIOUS POVERTY

We must begin, teaches Teresa, with exterior detachment, letting go of our attachment to material possessions. Again, the problem is not so much in possessions as it is our attachment to them, our possession by them. Religious vows of poverty can help with this detachment, but such vows are not essential to, nor are they a guarantee of, the true spirit of detachment that must

> The problem is not so much in possessions as it is our attachment to them, our possession by them.

occur: "I do not call 'giving up everything' entering religious life, for there can be impediments to entering religious life, and the perfect soul can be detached and humble anywhere; although this latter may involve greater trial, for being in a monastery is a big help" (W 12.5). In fact, as she knew from experience, being in a cloister does not necessarily free one from the "world." Men and women religious can simply live according to worldly values even in the cloister in perhaps less obvious but nonetheless real ways (L 7.3–5; IC 3.1.4).

A spirit of poverty is a critically important value for Teresa.[3] She had hoped to found all of her monasteries in complete poverty, that is, without a steady, fixed income from such sources as

---

3. Tomás Alvarez, *Comentarios a las obras de Santa Teresa: Libro de la vida, Camino de perfección, Castillo interior* (Burgos, Spain: Editorial Monte Carmelo, 2005), 293–95.

rent from land holdings (L 35). The second chapter of *The Way of Perfection* is devoted to this topic as she explains the essential rationale for her reform. Her commitment to poverty is rooted fundamentally in her reading of the Gospel and in the teaching and witness of Jesus who was born in a stable and died without anything on the cross (W 2.9). But external poverty, for Teresa, has only an instrumental value. In this way, it is virtually the same as her commitment to detachment from things. The real value of poverty is the freedom, the self-dominion, and ultimately the joy that it brings. Those especially who are vowed to it must live that commitment in spirit and in fact (W 2.5). Anything less is to live a lie—which Teresa so detests.

But Teresa's fundamental message here is not directed solely to religious. Today, many people are striving to live simply and in doing so, like Christ, to identify with those who have little. This too requires and nurtures a great spirit of detachment, given the prevailing messages of our culture concerning our "need" for more and better. In our contemporary world, many men and women, together with Pope Francis in his encyclical on the environment, *Laudato Si'*, are embracing a simpler lifestyle that seeks to protect the earth and its precious resources. Renouncing unnecessary possessions to join Christ in his solidarity with the poor and refusing to engage in practices that harm God's good creation and those who depend on it can also be liberating paths to the true detachment that frees us more truly to love God and neighbor. This too is an authentic reading of the demands of the Gospel and a path to freedom from "worldly" values.

DETACHMENT AND MORTIFICATION

Also closely related to detachment is the theme of mortification. As its linguistic root suggests, mortification is about "putting to death," in this case, putting to death our attachments to the things of this world. Generally, Teresa uses the word "mortification" to refer to the reform of *internal* attitudes and the term "penances" to refer to *external* practices of self-denial and observances.[4] True mortification is more about acting against our erring desires and gradually bringing them into line with that for which our spirit most authentically yearns: "This interior mortification is acquired, as I said, by proceeding gradually, not giving in to our own will and appetites, even in little things, until the body is completely surrendered to the spirit" (W 12.1). Mortification is therefore the effort to attain a greater freedom by actively working against our inordinate desires and attachments that obstruct our freedom. The Lenten practice of "giving something up for Lent" and practicing some form of self-denial can be a type of mortification that seeks to make us more faithful Christians once Lent is over.

It is interesting to note that in *The Way of Perfection*, in which Teresa is laying out her essential teaching about the path to the deepest prayer, she has almost nothing to say about penitential practices, despite the fact that such corporal penances were very characteristic of her time and religious culture. In fact, she urges that the penitential practices prescribed generally by the church and by the order are sufficient. More focus on penances can be a distraction from what matters more deeply and can even become a source of warped pride in one's ability to practice such penances (W 10.6; 15.3; 39.3).

In the *Life*, Teresa recounts, with obvious admiration, the extreme mortifications and penances of her contemporary, the great Franciscan ascetic St. Peter of Alcántara (L 27.16–20). She tells us, for example, that he went for forty years with only an

---

4. Herráiz, *Solo Dios Basta*, 151, 154.

hour and a half of sleep each night—and then while sitting up and resting his head on a log that he had nailed to the wall. He went barefoot in summer and winter. He ate every third day. For three years, he never raised his head so that he had never seen the faces of the friars with whom he lived. Such are the penances that were held up by the spirituality of the day, and Teresa obviously thinks highly of it. But she never recommends it. Instead, she says succinctly, "There are many ways . . . of trampling on the world" (L 27.16).

Teresa's focus is on internal renewal and freedom. Even in her *Constitutions*, *The Manner of Making the Visitation*, and in her letters, it is clear that her concern is on interior conversion over external practices and observances. On her first trip to the first foundation of the male branch of the reform (whose first members included St. John of the Cross), she praised their spirit of mortification but expressed concern over their excessive penances (F 14.11, 12). And later, in a letter to Carmelite friar Ambrosio Mariano she says, "Understand, Father, that I am fond of strictness in the practice of virtue but not of austerity" (Ltr 161.8).[5]

DETACHMENT FROM FAMILY

Teresa is surprisingly adamant about the need for detachment from family: "Oh, if we religious could understand the great harm that comes from having too much to do with relatives!" (W 9.1). "I am astonished," she continues, "by the harm that is caused from dealing with relatives. . . . I don't know what it is in the world that we renounce when we say that we give up everything for God if we don't give up the main thing, namely,

---

5. Ibid.,148–63.

our relatives" (W 9.2). For her, inordinate attachment to family is a fundamental issue: "Well, believe me, our relatives are what clings to us most from the world, as I have said, and the most difficult to detach ourselves from" (W 9.5). Obviously, statements such as these require further explanation for people of today!

While it is true that Teresa's insistence on this issue is best understood as directed to cloistered religious and in the historical context of her religious culture, she is making a deeper point here about the work of detachment. Teresa is concerned that all of our relationships be consistent with and serve our growing communion with God. Precisely because our relationship with family members is natural, it can be easier unconsciously to mask an element of neediness or to justify the kind of interactions that actually obstruct the attainment of our life's goal rather than help it. We can speak, for example, of codependent relationships, family members (and friends!) who are "enablers" of unhealthy or bad behaviors, and people whose genuine love for one another is marked by as much neediness as selfless loving. Both friends and family members can be a bad example to us, draw us into superficial or even unworthy conversations, or drag us down emotionally, morally, or spiritually (W 20.4). Such unhealthiness can be part of any relationship. Sometimes it is more difficult to see, admit, and free oneself when it involves family members.

We live in a world today in which we probably have far less contact with extended family members than in Teresa of Avila's world. We often no longer live near family members as adults. We are more influenced by a much wider variety of people and factors beyond our families than was the case in Teresa's time and culture. And still, Teresa is offering fundamental insights about the ways that relationships, familial and all the rest, can help or hinder us.

In fact, Teresa had a great love for her own family, and she continued to keep in contact with them throughout her life. At the same time, she had seen in her early religious life at the Monastery of the Incarnation that involvement with family could be a serious obstacle to the life of the spirit. The nuns at the monastery of her profession spent a great deal of time in the community's visiting parlors, chatting and gossiping with family. This had been one of her own favorite pastimes. Since that cash-strapped monastery depended so much on the donations from wealthy family members, the practice was something of a necessity—a kind of "donor relations." But such conversations did nothing positive in a spiritual way for the nuns or for their relatives. They were a distraction and a constant temptation to the nuns to think according to the ways of the secular world outside the monastery. Rather than bringing family members into closer relationship to God, such interaction often drew the nuns to focus on the "vanities" of the world.

At a deeper level, what Teresa is opposing is a self-centered attachment to people. Friends and family can be important companions on the spiritual journey, as Teresa urged her nuns to be for one another. On the other hand, they can also be distractions from one's fundamental love for God. Rather than loving people in God, we can love them more than God or instead of God. Or we can place them alongside God, trying to love them and to love God on the same plane. It is easy enough to love other people at least partially for what they can do for us: entertain and distract us, make us feel secure, affirm us, and so forth. But what we need to do is to love others freely, for themselves, and for their spiritual benefit. We need to love them in God, with God's love.

What would Teresa of Avila make of the very contemporary dilemma of so many adults (including religious) who must now devote a great deal of time and attention to care of elderly parents? This is a very modern predicament. People are living longer at the same time that we now lack close-knit extended families who can share in the duties of elder care. It must be noted first of all that Teresa viewed commitment to parents as a fundamental value. She exempted them from her caution about attachment to relatives: "By relatives I do not mean parents, for parents very seldom fail to help their children, and it is right for us to console them in their need. Let us not remain aloof from them if we see that communicating with them does not harm our religious life. This communication can be carried on with detachment; and so too, with brothers and sisters" (W 9.3). Furthermore, care of elderly parents can constitute a true selflessness that has little to do with attachment and everything to do with a true selfless love. The very real challenge of such care—in the midst of the rest of life's responsibilities and demands—can be very much a path to a deeper self-forgetful love. And this is the true purpose of detachment.

DETACHMENT FROM OUR OWN BODILY "NEEDS"

As we have already mentioned, Teresa was not greatly concerned for bodily penances. Her asceticism, especially in her historical and cultural context, was decidedly moderate. At the same time, though, she saw that it is all too easy to be too concerned with our physical comfort: "A fault this body has is that the more comfort we try to give it the more needs it discovers. It's amazing how much comfort it wants" (W 11.2). Apparently, things haven't changed that much since the sixteenth century! We need detachment from our self-indulgent desire for comfort and even from an excessive concern for our health. (This is the subject of chapters 10 and 11 of *The*

Way of Perfection.) Teresa tells us that the challenge is not to embrace harsh penances but rather to refuse to give into the whims and excessive "needs" of the body and its demands. This is essential to the authentic self-dominion that is part of a true freedom: "For little by little as we grow accustomed to this attitude, we shall, with the Lord's help, remain lords of our bodies" (W 11.5).

Teresa argues that we can also be overly concerned with our physical health when it comes, for example, to fasting (W 10.5). Perhaps even more today, some of us are afraid to fast too seriously because it might affect our health. Depending on the type of fasting under consideration (not unlike unhealthy contemporary diet fads), concern for our health might be well taken, and Teresa was not one to advocate any practice that would seriously hamper our health. But sometimes concern about physical health can be excessive in relation to other important values. The Catholic tradition lauds the virtue of temperance, which helps us to choose—in matters of eating and sleeping, for example—in a balanced way that promotes our health. But the same tradition teaches us that there is also a parallel infused (divinely given) virtue of temperance that allows us to judge what constitutes a genuinely healthy balance in light of other important and even higher values. Fasting, prayer vigils, and late-night eucharistic adoration may not make sense to a purely human temperance, but to true Christian temperance they can make perfect sense (at the right time and in the right way).

In a similar way, Teresa notes that a little illness can too easily lead us to complain: "It seems to me an imperfection, my Sisters, to be always complaining about light illnesses. If you can tolerate them, don't complain about them. . . . If someone is truly sick, she should say so and take the necessary remedy" (W 11.1). In fact, we can be quite self-indulgent about little illnesses.

It is so easy to tell ourselves that "I have a headache" so I can't be expected to pray or even to go to Mass—even though I am well enough to watch television or go out to eat with friends. Teresa says, almost as a parody, "Hardly does our head begin to ache than we stop going to choir [i.e., to the monastery's common liturgical prayer], which won't kill us either. We stay away one day because our head ached, another because it was just now aching, and three more so that it won't ache again" (W 10.6).[6]

Teresa is cautioning us that we can get our values out of their proper order. A legitimate concern for health can easily become an obsession or at least an overriding value. An authentic need to restrict our activities because of physical discomfort can sometimes be easily overridden for activities that we enjoy but not for activities that are in fact more important. As Teresa is saying, we can become attached to our health and comfort in a way that obstructs our freedom to do what is right and thereby to grow in love for God.

Teresa reminds her nuns that they came to the monastery in order to die (W 10.5), and they should see their concern for health in that context. We could take that comment purely as hyperbole to a group of supremely dedicated nuns, but it really speaks to the deeper fear that undergirds

> Teresa tells us that the challenge is not to embrace harsh penances but rather to refuse to give into the whims and excessive "needs" of the body and its demands.

6. The Kavanaugh edition of Teresa's collected works has included the last sentence, just quoted, from an earlier edition of *The Way of Perfection*, that Teresa edited out of the later edition.

much of our concern about our health—that is, the fear of death and dying. Underlying our overconcern for our health and bodies is the fear of death, which is part of the human condition, in the sixteenth century as well as today. Our life is a precious gift from God, and we are its stewards. But physical health and life in these material bodies are passing. It is not part of our responsible stewardship to be overly attached to our physical living, nor to the fear of dying. In an age and culture that places so much value on youth and the maintenance of our physical health and conditioning—that devotes immense resources to the technology that prolongs life and delays dying—Teresa's challenge to be detached even from health, the body, and physical life is timely and necessary.[7]

FROM EXTERIOR TO INTERIOR

Teresa makes an important distinction between exterior and interior detachment. In regard to external things, we must often decide consciously and immediately to detach ourselves from our possessions, whether getting rid of them or at least creating some distance from them. This is what Teresa means by mortification. The interior work of detachment is more difficult and can take considerably more time, but it is precisely this internal letting go that is the true detachment. As we have said, the issue is not possessions in themselves as much as it is an attitude of possessiveness. The concern is about the reality of being possessed by things rather than simply possessing them.

In the end, the true challenge is to become detached from ourselves, that is, from what is merely superficial or false in ourselves and thus the root of our attachments to external

---

7. Alvarez, *Comentarios*, 331–32.

superficialities. Even having become detached from things outside of ourselves, from physical things including our health and
physical life as well as our family and other needy loves, we must
still face our attachment to self. We can cling to a false kind
of self. The real enemy is not outside of us. It is within us. It is
us. Teresa says that we can view our detachment from external
things as having successfully locked out the thieves who would
break into our houses and steal our precious inner freedom.
Arriving at such detachment would be a genuine accomplishment, but she warns us that it should not leave us feeling secure.
The real problem is that the worse thief of all is still in the house,
and that thief is us:

> By feeling secure you would resemble someone who very
> tranquilly lies down after having locked his doors for fear of
> thieves while allowing the thieves to remain inside the house.
> And you already know that there is no worse thief than we
> ourselves. For if you do not walk very carefully and if each Sis-
> ter is not alert in going against her own will as though doing
> so were more important than all else, there are many things
> that will take away this holy freedom of spirit by which you
> can fly to your Maker without being held down by clay or
> leaden feet. (W 10.1)

Again, detachment is ultimately God's work in us. Teresa
herself prays dramatically that God will free her from herself
and so liberate her liberty: "Don't punish me by giving me what
I want or desire if Your love, which lives in me always, doesn't
desire it. May this 'I' die, and may another live in me greater than
I and better for me than I, so that I may serve Him. May He live
and give me life. May He reign, and may I be captive, for my
soul doesn't want any other liberty. How can he be free who is a
stranger to the Most High?" (S 17.3).

Again, the world is not the enemy. The external element of the struggle is against what Teresa calls the "vanities of the world" (*las vanidades del mundo*) or the vain world (*el mundo vano*). She sees clearly how she herself pursued just such vanities in earlier life (L 7.1; 7.14; 7.17). These empty things are part of the "lie." But she came to see that the real foe is internal—not the vanities of the world but the vanity that we ourselves are. "We are vanity itself" (*somos la misma vanidad*), she concludes (IC 1.2.5).

Detachment from ourselves is closely linked with that other necessary virtue, humility. Pride, concern for "honor," and quickness to take offense are really types of attachment to ourselves that must be opposed by humility. The title of chapter 10 of *The Way of Perfection* is "How it is not enough to be detached from what was mentioned [i.e., created things and family] if we are not detached from ourselves, and how both this virtue of detachment and humility go together." We are involved in "a war against ourselves" (W 12.1). We can also say that attachment to ourselves is an obvious hindrance to authentic self-giving in love. We therefore need, in addition to detachment and humility, the third of the three necessary virtues: love for neighbor and for one another.

In our struggle against attachment, as with our pursuit of humility, we must not deceive ourselves about our progress. Teresa urges vigilance and a self-critical gaze (in a positive sense of "self-critical"). She warns against being detached merely in words or self-opinion rather than in fact and in deed (L 21.7). Here again we meet the danger of concern for honor: "Not all those of us who think we are detached, are in fact; it is necessary not to grow careless in this matter. Let any person who wants to advance and yet feels concerned about some point of honor believe me and strive to overcome this attachment, which is like a chain that cannot be broken by any file but only by God through our prayer and earnest cooperation" (L 31.20). In the end, we must pursue, with God's help, a complete detachment that will eliminate any hindrance to our freedom. As John of the Cross puts it, it matters little if a bird is tied by a thin thread or by a strong cord. In either case, it is prevented from flying (*The Ascent of Mount Carmel*, 1.11.4).

WE ARE ALREADY RICH

Teresa's insistence on detachment is rooted in her boundless loving desire for God. Excessive or disordered attachment to things, to family, to the body, to honor, to self—all of these are distractions and obstacles to attaining communion with her Beloved. Detachment, in that sense, is grounded in the awakening of a desire that is deeper, more profound, than our yearning for merely worldly things. The work of detachment is born of a desire for an infinite good and promise. This is the desire that is fed by prayer and deepening encounter with God.

From another perspective, Teresa tells us, detachment is grounded in a recognition of what we already possess—riches far beyond the vanities to which we so often find ourselves attached. If, on the other hand, we were more truly aware of what is already ours in God and of what God holds out to us, the work of detachment from what is infinitely less than God would be so much easier: "For how can people benefit and share their gifts lavishly if they do not understand that they are rich? . . . We are so miserable and so inclined to earthly things that those who do not understand they have a pledge of heavenly things will find it hard to abhor in fact and with detachment everything here below" (L 10.6). Or, as she says even more beautifully, "What helps is that the soul embrace the good Jesus our Lord with determination, for since in Him everything is found, in Him everything is forgotten" (W 9.5). Or again, as her bookmark says, "Whoever has God lacks nothing. God alone is enough."

It is precisely the increasing awareness of our blessings and of God's promises for deepening communion that come to propel the work of detachment. This is true especially but not exclusively with mystical graces. Following a vision of Christ, she comments on how the experience gave her freedom from her attachment to a needy love for others: "After I beheld the extraordinary beauty of the Lord, I didn't see anyone who in comparison with Him seemed to attract me or occupy my thoughts" (L 37.4). In describing the deeper mystical graces of the sixth dwelling places in *The Interior Castle*, she says, "And while the spirit is far outside itself, from all it can understand, great things are shown to it. When it again senses that it is within itself, the benefits it feels are remarkable, and it has so little esteem for all earthly things in comparison to the things it has seen that the former seem like dung" (IC 6.5.9).

God is our true treasure, infinitely more precious than anything this world has to offer. The more we recognize and experience this truth, the more we will see reality as it is and the easier it will be to detach ourselves from anything that is less than God. We will become free to love God, other people, ourselves, and the created world with the liberty of God's children.

6

HUMILITY:
TO WALK IN TRUTH

The virtue of humility, according to Teresa, is essential for attaining union with God. It is a key to the ascetical foundation of her spirituality: "Since this edifice is built entirely on humility, the closer one comes to God the more progress there must be in this virtue; and if there is no progress in humility, everything is going to be ruined" (L 12.4; also L 22.11; IC 7.4.8).[1] Humility is, in fact, so central that, in introducing the three necessary virtues that we are examining, Teresa notes that humility can actually be seen as the "main practice," which embraces the other two (W 4.4).

For Teresa, humility is both the foundation and the fruit of prayer.[2] Authentic prayer is necessarily grounded in humility (L 10.5; L 22.11; W 17.1). This is because growth in prayer, especially in contemplative prayer, is a gift. While we can develop a strong habit of prayer and dispose ourselves for yet deeper prayer,

---

1. Maximiliano Herráiz, "La Humildad es Andar en Verdad," in *A zaga de tu huella: Escritos teresiano-sanjuanistas y espiritualidad* (Burgos, Spain: Editorial Monte Carmelo, 2004), 249; Jesús Castellano, "Espiritualidad teresiana: Experiencia y doctrina," in *Introducción a la lectura de Santa Teresa*, ed. Alberto Barrientos (Madrid: Editorial de Espiritualidad, 2002), 253; Félix Málax, "Humildad," in *Diccionario de Santa Teresa*, ed. Tomás Alvarez, 2nd ed. (Burgos, Spain: Editorial Monte Carmelo, 2006), 348; Secundino Castro, *Ser Cristiano según Santa Teresa: Teología y espiritualidad*, 2nd ed. (Madrid: Editorial de Espiritualidad, 1985), 317.

2. Herráiz, "La Humildad," 264.

true contemplation can only be given to us by God. Our attitude then must be humility, trusting that God will dispose all things (including our advance into deeper forms of prayer) for our good. At the same time, for Teresa, true prayer always bears fruit in a deeper humility (W 39.7; L 17.3; L 20.7). In fact, growth in humility is one of the surest signs of any authentic encounter with God. Without it, whatever one has experienced, it was not God. This is most especially true of profound mystical graces (L 15.10; L 15.14; L 17.3; L 19.2; L 20.29; L 28.9; W 17.3).

Teresa's teaching on humility is rich and deep. Because of its essential place in her thought—as the central virtue of the three necessary virtues—it is important to examine it in some detail. Frankly, many people today would not consider humility to be among life's most fundamental of virtues. In our day, it might be easy enough to assume that her emphasis here is culturally bound or perhaps directed exclusively to those in religious life. Would she alter her basic message if she were to address us today, or is her teaching on humility simply a relic of a bygone day? In order to respond to that question, we must try to understand Teresa's teaching in its original context—as we must do when we try to interpret the meaning and to appreciate the contemporary value of any historical text. This is certainly true in our reading of Teresa's teaching on this virtue, which she believes to be so essential to the Christian life and to the reception of contemplative prayer. Further, a closer examination of this context is a window into Teresa's cultural and religious world and into her personal and spiritual formation and development.

A FALSE HONOR

The culture of sixteenth-century Spain placed a great value on honor (*honra*): one's personal honor, the honor of one's good name, and the honor of one's family. With such concerns came, as well, attention to perceived slights, offenses, and oversights. Such an attitude is probably not absent from any culture or time, but in the world in which Teresa was raised, its importance was virtually paramount, especially for the people of the upper classes and those concerned with upward mobility. As a very young woman, Teresa herself was concerned about questions of honor—and attention to her family's honor may have helped to keep her out of adolescent trouble (L 2.3, 7)—but the mature Teresa reacted strongly against it. For her, it is the very opposite of the humility that she understands to be utterly essential to the authentic Christian life.

Concern for honor was based in the rigid hierarchy of feudal culture, still present in sixteenth-century Europe. In Spain, historical circumstances resulted in an even greater attention to it, often linked with concern for "purity of blood" (*pureza de sangre*).[3] Until the end of the fifteenth century, the three great religions of Christianity, Judaism, and Islam had lived a sometimes uneasy but largely workable coexistence on the Iberian Peninsula. All of that changed in 1492 when the famous King Ferdinand and Queen Isabella—in addition to funding Christopher Columbus's "discovery" of the Americas—defeated the last Islamic kingdom of Granada and expelled the Jews from Spain (or, as their only alternative, forced the Jews to convert to Christianity). It is from this latter circumstance of conversions that concerns about "purity of blood" were added to traditional feudal class distinctions. It became a point of honor to belong

---

3. Daniel de Pablo Maroto, "*Camino de Perfección*," in *Introducción a la lectura de Santa Teresa*, ed. Alberto Barrientos (Madrid: Editorial de Espiritualidad, 2002), 453–55. For more information on the contemporary world of St. Teresa, see Tomás Alvarez, *St. Teresa of Avila: 100 Themes on Her Life and Work*, trans. Kieran Kavanaugh, 1–44 (Washington, D.C.: ICS Publications, 2011).

to a family that not only had a long and noble lineage but also had been consistently Christian, without "taint" of Muslim or Jewish blood. This concern later became linked with the concern of the Spanish Inquisition to root out remaining Jewish beliefs and practices that were suspected in those who had only recently—and perhaps only for convenience or out of necessity—converted to Christianity (called *conversos*).

But where there's a will, there's a way. Even in a society so vigilant about such things, status and respectability could be bought from a cash-strapped Spanish crown (even if a whiff of suspicion or disdain would still remain). Many *converso* families, such as Teresa's own, could move from one part of Spain to another where their familial roots in Judaism were not known. And in fact, if they had the economic means, they could even buy their way into the lower nobility, which Teresa's own father and uncles did in 1523 when she was eight years old.[4]

Concerns about honor and purity of blood inevitably entered as well into ecclesiastical structures and religious orders. In fact, just as individuals known to be from *converso* families could be denied promotion in Spanish society in general and in civil structures, mixed blood could also prevent one from admission to some religious communities. Such concern for class distinction and family lineage made a great deal of difference in religious communities of the time. When Teresa entered the Monastery of the Incarnation in Avila in 1535, she was entitled to be addressed as "Doña" (Lady) Teresa, and the nuns of her social class and above could expect to have better rooms, food, and religious habits as well as servants, depending on their family's class and financial means. Meanwhile, the nuns from more modest families and means might live in dormitories and suffer

---

4. Alvarez, *St. Teresa of Avila*, 67–70.

hardships, depending on the economic fortunes of the monastery. In that world, even in the context of devout religious life, it did not seem out of place to take serious offense at not being addressed or treated in accord with one's rank in the wider society.

In the Carmelite reform, initiated by Teresa, the title of "Doña" was to be dropped—along with all trappings of the class distinctions that ruled society outside the walls of the monastery. "Purity of blood" was not a requisite for admission. For her, all of these trappings fell under the pejorative sense of her use of the term *honra*—or more specifically, *la negra honra* or *negros puntos de honra* [literally, "black" honor or "black" points of honor—or, in more contemporary form, "corrupt" honor] (W 36.6, 7). In this, Teresa's reform can rightly be seen as a social criticism of her contemporary culture, and her criticism is scathing: "If our [heavenly] Father had not so much majesty, it wouldn't surprise me if we refused to be known as His children. The world has come to such a state that if the father is of a lower status than his son, the son doesn't feel honored in recognizing him as his father" (W 27.5).

Some commentators have conjectured that part of Teresa's rejection of the concept of honor and its trappings was rooted in her own family history. The Jewish roots of her family were unknown after her death and not rediscovered until 1946. Her paternal grandfather, Juan Sanchéz, a wealthy merchant in Toledo, was accused of returning to his Jewish roots and was publically "reconciled" by the Inquisition in 1485.[5] This history was certainly known to her family, and once relocated to Avila, they had consciously tried to separate themselves from

---

5. Maroto, "*Camino*," 453–55. See also Tomás Alvarez, "Honra," in *Diccionario de Santa Teresa*, ed. Tomás Alvarez, 2nd ed. (Burgos, Spain: Editorial Monte Carmelo, 2006), 336–37.

this past. Perhaps then it is no surprise that the tension of living under this cloud might make Teresa react against these rigid class structures. The inner world of a strict cloister would allow a separation from these wider societal concerns, and her sound rejection of it could be seen as an expression of her personal abhorrence of the expectations under which she and her family had had to live.

At the same time, without denying that her own situation might have contributed to her disdain, a simple reading of her works makes it abundantly clear that Teresa's strong and constant opposition to concern for honor runs far deeper, into her fundamental beliefs about the foundations of any true Christian life and prayer. Concern for honor was the very opposite of humility, one of the virtues that Teresa—as so many other spiritual teachers in our tradition have taught—judged as simply essential to any path to genuine prayer and holiness. For Teresa, one cannot grow in prayer without rooting out such concern, while at the same time, perfect prayer casts out all consideration of things such as worldly honor of any sort (W 12.5).

The word *honra* appears about forty times in *The Way of Perfection* in which, as its title suggests, Teresa devotes the most sustained attention to the steps that lead to the life of union with God.[6] Although she sometimes uses the term in a positive way—speaking, for example, of God's honor (L 21.1; IC 6.1.4, 7.3.2)—most often her use is negative, at times decidedly so. She explicitly devotes two of the book's forty-two chapters (chaps. 12 and 27) to the topic, though it is discussed in a number of

---

6. Jurek Nawojowski, "El problema del honor en *Camino de Perfección*," in *Camino de Perfección de Santa Teresa de Jesús: Actas del II Congreso Internacional Teresiano en preparación del V centenario de su nacimiento (1515–2015)*, ed. Javier Sancho Fermín and Romulo Cuartas Lodoño (Burgos, Spain: Editorial Monte Carmelo, 2012), 358n2. Nawojowski notes that the word *honra* therefore appears more times than many terms that would be considered essential to a serious discussion of the spiritual life—words such as virtue, friendship, or poverty.

other places in the work. Teresa never provides a formal definition of *honra*, but in sixteenth-century usage, in negative terms,
it meant the estimation and respect for one's own dignity, a high
opinion of oneself, the personal sense of fame that comes with
merit or accomplishment, or the sense or demonstration of one's
own self-esteem.[7]

According to Teresa, a sense of *honra* in her culture depended
on three foundations.[8] The first was money:

> In my opinion honor and money almost always go together;
> anyone who wants honor doesn't despise money, and any-
> one who despises money doesn't care much about honor. Let
> this be clearly understood, for it seems to me that the desire
> for honor always brings with it some interest in money or
> income. It would be a wonder if any poor person were hon-
> ored in the world; on the contrary, even if he may be wor-
> thy of honor, he is little esteemed. True poverty brings with
> it overwhelming honor. Poverty that is chosen for God alone
> has no need of pleasing anyone but Him. (W 2.6)

The second foundation of *honra* were offices and titles
that were believed to merit special treatment for their bearers.
Clearly, in a rigidly hierarchical society such as existed in Spain at
the time, aristocratic and ecclesiastical titles and offices brought
expected honor, but Teresa's strongest critique involves the trans-
posing of such concerns to religious life. In her commentary on
the Our Father in *The Way of Perfection*, as she reflects on the
phrase "forgive us as we forgive," she notes the seemingly unfor-
givable little slights and offenses that can occur in a religious
community. Perhaps, she suggests, Jesus included the petition

---

7. Ibid., 357–58, citing the dictionary of the Real Academia Española.
8. Ibid., 359–60.

about forgiving others precisely because he knew that his follow-
ers are so fond of "this miserable honor" (W 36.7). Her comments on concern for academic and ecclesiastical titles and rank
are both scathing and wonderfully ironic:

> But consider, Sisters, that the devil hasn't forgotten us. He
> also invents his own honors in monasteries and establishes his
> own laws. There, people ascend and descend in rank just as in
> the world. Those with degrees must follow in order, accord-
> ing to their academic titles. Why? I don't know. The one who
> has managed to become a professor of theology must not
> descend to professor of philosophy, for it is a point of honor
> that he must ascend and not descend. Even if obedience
> should command, he would consider the change an affront.
> And there will always be someone standing by to defend him
> and tell him that it's an insult; then the devil at once discloses
> reasons why even according to God's law this thinking seems
> right. Well, now, among ourselves: the one who has been pri-
> oress must remain ineligible for any lower office; a preoccupa-
> tion about who the senior is—for we never forget this—and
> we even think at times we gain merit by such concern because
> the order commands it. (W 36.4)

She concludes in the paragraph that follows, "One doesn't
know whether to laugh or to cry; the latter would be more fitting" (W 36.5).

Age and seniority in the community are the third possible foundation of false honor: "Take careful note of interior
stirrings, especially if they have to do with privileges of rank.
God, by His Passion, deliver us from dwelling on such words
or thoughts as 'I have seniority,' 'I am older,' 'I have done more
work,' 'the other is better treated than I.' If such thoughts come
they should be quickly cut off" (W 12.4).

In contrast, Teresa calls on her readers to be concerned for the honor of God. Moreover, she challenges us to recall that our God accepted dishonor on our behalf: "O Lord, Lord! Are you our Model and Master? Yes, indeed! Well, then, what did Your honor consist of, You who honored us? Didn't You indeed lose it in being humiliated unto death? No, Lord, but You won it for all" (W 36.5).

Reflecting the fact that in her contemporary culture a wife would necessarily share in the honor or dishonor of her spouse,[9] Teresa urges her nuns to embrace dishonor—paying no mind to seeming slights, overlooking little offenses, accepting in most circumstances blame without defense—in imitation and in conformity to their true Spouse. In this way, they will attain true and lasting honor, sharing in the authentic honor of their Spouse (W 13.2). She is emphatic and clear in her admonition:

> You should run a thousand miles from such expressions as: "I was right." "They had no reason for doing this to me." "The one who did this to me was wrong." God deliver us from this poor way of reasoning. Does it seem right that our good Jesus suffered so many insults and was made to undergo so much injustice? I don't know why the nun who doesn't want to carry the cross, except the one that seems to her reasonable, is in the monastery. . . . What kind of reasoning is this? I certainly don't understand it. . . . I don't know what there is to talk about. Either we are brides of so great a King or we are not. (W 13.1–2)

"If she bears dishonor as it must be borne, she will not be without honor in this life or the next" (W 13.3). In effect, concern

---

9. In fact, in a brief account of her experience of spiritual marriage, she says that God told her, "From now on not only will you look after My honor as being the honor of your Creator, King, and God, but you will look after it as My true bride. My honor is yours, and yours Mine" (ST 31).

for honor undermines one's configuration to Christ, who was humble and self-forgetful.[10]

Ultimately, concern for superficial honor cannot coexist with real spiritual growth: "The soul's profit and what the world calls honor can never go together" (W 36.3). It is simply not possible for the person who loves such vanities as worldly honor truly to love God (W 40.3). What a sad world it is, she laments, in which people pay no attention to their inner life but are so concerned with something so superficial as external regard (W 22.5). "God deliver us," she says, "from persons who are concerned about honor while trying to serve Him. Consider it an evil gain, and, as I said, honor is itself lost by desiring it, especially in matters of rank. For there is no toxin in the world that kills perfection as do these things" (W 12.7). On this point, she is adamant: "But believe me in one thing: if there is any vain esteem of honor or wealth (and this can be had inside monasteries as well as outside, although inside the occasions for it are more removed and the fault would be greater), you will never grow very much or come to enjoy the true fruit of prayer. And this is so even though you may have many years of experience in prayer—or, better, I should say reflection because perfect prayer in the end removes these bad habits" (W 12.5).

It is the devil, she opines, who sometimes makes Christians think they are in fact obliged to receive honor. But the very idea of embracing such worldly honor is a like a caterpillar that eats away at the tree so that it cannot flourish and cannot give the

---

10. Alvarez, "Honra," 345–46. In another work, the same author notes that in the original Spanish title of chapter 13 of *The Way of Perfection*, Teresa is playing on two different uses of the Spanish word *razón*: one must flee from the world's maxims and rules (*puntos y razones del mundo*, i.e., the world's foolish rules that protect honor) and true wisdom (*la verdadera razón*) that cares nothing for honor. Tomás Alvarez, *Comentarios a las obras de Santa Teresa: Libro de la vida, Camino de perfección, Castillo interior* (Burgos, Spain: Editorial Monte Carmelo, 2005), 340.

fruit of good example to others, or it is like an organ whose tuning or timing is off and thus produces music that is dissonant (L 31.20–21). The person who experiences authentic contemplation, on the other hand, does not care about the esteem of others—in fact, is more comfortable with dishonor than with honor. Such concern in a person would be a sure sign that his or her experience was not truly of God (W 36.8–12).

Beyond its detrimental impact on our individual lives, the great religious founder and reformer cautions that concerns for honor and attention to slights and offenses undermine authentic Christian community life. More than a lack of strict observance, things such as concern for points of honor are the "main evil in monasteries" (W 7.10). Rather than promoting unity and harmony in a community, concern for honor and its attending attention to slights and taking offense undermine community relations and focus attention on the individual—and on what is really superficial and even false for her or him.[11]

A Word for Today

At first glance, Teresa's frequent critique of this concern for honor might in our own day seem arcane, restricted in its value to a very different culture than ours. As we cautioned in speaking of the selflessness of authentic love, in our day, we must note that sometimes there may be value in standing up for important rights in respect for our own inherent human dignity and for the good of others. But even reading Teresa's thoughts on humility with contemporary eyes, it remains true that she is reflecting on a profound human reality and deep-seated human tendency. Her teaching therefore contains

---

11. Maroto, "*Camino*," 456.

enduring lessons for Christians of today who want to attain a deep relationship with God and to promote authentic Christian community.

While we do not experience concern for "purity of blood," concerns about reputation, status, and prestige are not foreign to us. We can still feel slighted or offended in the workplace or in social relations. Contemporary consumerism and materialism often seek not only personal satisfaction and comfort but also the desire to "keep up with" or "get ahead" of others. Modern men and women are still quite capable of comparing themselves to others on the most superficial grounds, whether appearance, salary, possessing the latest gadgets, the size of their homes, or the neighborhood in which they live. In our encounters with others, we can sometimes glimpse in ourselves an otherwise unconscious attention to class differences and levels of education. And concern about titles and rank in ecclesiastical and religious life is also not foreign to us. Modern prelates, priests, and religious can take offense at not being recognized, addressed properly, or being asked to do something that they consider is not deemed fitting to their rank. Men and women in every walk of life are quite capable of feeling offended or slighted in their relationships with coworkers, neighbors, and even family. Sometimes, if we are honest with ourselves, we can see that our umbrage or resentment really borders on the petty and is more a reflection of our insecurities than something worth a further thought.

In traditional piety, all of this would probably fall under terms such as "seeking after human respect" or "pride." But whatever we call it, Teresa is right to see it as superficial and ultimately as simply false to what it means to be a Christian and, in fact, false to what it means to be authentically human before God. In contemporary terms, we might say she is talking about the false constructs by which we try to fashion, protect, and promote a false image of ourselves. What she calls "honor" is the name for the ways we seek merely external, superficial, and ultimately false ways to protect our sometimes shallow and fragile egos.

Teresa's challenge to cast aside concern for worldly honor and to be ready to embrace worldly dishonor is the fundamental Christian necessity to embrace the "folly of the cross" (1 Cor 1:18–31). The world's (in the negative sense of the word) values are not values at all. They are sometimes disvalues. The world's honor is ultimately no honor at all. To be conformed and united to

> In our encounters with others, we can sometimes glimpse in ourselves an otherwise unconscious attention to class differences and levels of education.

Christ crucified, humiliated, and dishonored in this world is the truest honor of all. This is the "logic of the cross."

HUMILITY IS TO WALK IN TRUTH

> [The soul] deplores the time in which it was concerned about its reputation and deplores the deception it suffered in believing that what the world called honor was honor. It sees how this belief about honor is the greatest lie and that all of us are involved with it. It understands that authentic honor stands not with falsehood but with truth, judging what is something to be something, and what is nothing to be nothing, since everything that comes to an end is nothing and less than nothing and is not pleasing to God. (L 20.26)

For Teresa, to live with concern for worldly honor is to live a lie. It is to live in falsehood, under the spell of an illusion. Humility, on the other hand, is the opposite of and the cure for such falsehood. Humility is to walk in truth (*andar en verdad*) about God and about ourselves: "Once I was pondering why our Lord was so fond of this virtue of humility, and this thought came to me—in my opinion not as a result of reflection but suddenly: It is because God is supreme Truth; and to be humble is to walk in truth, for it is a very deep truth that of ourselves we have nothing good but only misery and nothingness. Whoever does not understand this walks in falsehood [*anda en mentira*]" (IC 6.10.7).

True humility is grounded in the truth that is God. God, the creator all things and the one in whose image we are created, is the measure of our humanity. In this sense, God who is Truth is also the truth about men and women created in the divine image. And the Truth has been made flesh in Jesus who said of himself that he is "the Way, the Truth, and the Life" (Jn 14:6). Jesus Christ is the truth about God and, at one and the same time, the truth about authentic human living. Without sin or falsity of any kind, Jesus walked in truth. His life, example, and teaching are therefore the standard by which we must live.

Teresa's challenge to walk humbly in the truth then is a statement about the shape of authentic humanity and, at the same time, about our utterly essential relationship with Christ. It is one sign of Teresa's consistent Christocentrism. To walk in the truth is necessarily to walk the way of Jesus. Anything else is to walk in falsehood and lies.[12] No wonder that when the Inquisition banned virtually all books about recollection

---

12. Herráiz, "La Humildad," 253–55.

and prayer, Jesus responded to Teresa's distress by saying that he himself would be her truth: "His Majesty became the true book in which I saw all truths" (L 26.5). In a later vision, God was revealed to her as Truth itself, and God told her that all harm comes from not knowing the truths of the Scriptures and what they reveal (L 40.1–3). Failure to know the Scriptures is to be ignorant of the God who has there revealed the divine reality and thereby also to be ignorant of ourselves and how we ought to live.

The truth in which we must walk is twofold, both beautiful and tragic: that we are wonderfully created in the image of God and thus precious (IC 1.1.1) and, at the same time, that we are sinners and, on our own, undeserving and indeed nothing without God (IC 1.2).[13] That we are so wonderfully created should fill us with a humble sense of awe at what we have received. That we are sinners, standing always before the truth of God, should fill us with a constant sense of our need for God's mercy and help. It is only by walking daily in this twofold truth—growing in it—that we can live our humanity authentically and walk the path that leads to God. In the truth of who God is and who we are before God grows the humility to be open, receptive, and grateful for the gift of contemplation.

In reading Teresa, it is important to remember that this truth about ourselves is twofold. Her insistence on the need for constant attention to our misery and nothingness before God does not reflect a fundamentally negative anthropology, nor a sense of pessimism about humanity. She is equally insistent that we must remember how wonderfully we are made and the future to which we are called by God. To err on either side of this twofold

---

13. Málax, "Humilidad," 338–42.

truth is to live a lie about oneself, to live falsely, and to lose one's way in drawing close to God.

To know this reality—to walk in this truth—is, in some ways, the very heart of Teresa's teaching, perhaps even a summary in one phrase of her thought:[14] to know the truth of who God is and who we are before God establishes the conditions for a true relationship between us. It sets in motion the work of transformation in ourselves so we can live more faithfully the truth of what we are made and called to be, always aware both of our exalted calling and of our need. In this sense, Teresa's insight offers a profound anthropology and a path toward authentic human fulfillment. The human person is a history, an unfolding, of God's image in coming to know the truth, doing the truth, and walking in the truth.[15]

Jesus tells us in the Gospel that the truth will set us free (Jn 8:32), and Teresa's teaching on humility suggests an important way in which this statement is profoundly true. Our freedom, when we are blinded to the truth, cannot function as it should and cannot lead us where it should. Without a vision of the truth and a fundamental commitment to walk in that truth, we cannot make the right choices in our lives, pursue the right goals: "O free will, so much the slave of your freedom if you don't live fastened with fear and love of your Creator! Oh, when will that happy day arrive when you will see yourself drowned in the infinite sea of supreme truth, where you will no longer be free to sin!" (S 7.4).

But the logic of humility seems like foolishness to the world that lives the lie about things such as honor. The truth

---

14. This assertion is made by one of the most eminent contemporary Spanish commentators on Teresian thought in a classic study: Maximiliano Herráiz, *Solo Dios Basta: Claves de la espiritualidad teresiana*, 5th ed. (Madrid: Editorial de Espiritualidad, 2000), 195.

15. Herráiz, "La Humildad," 255.

of our humanity and the path to God cannot be found in the superficial, the passing, and the false. And yet, all of us live in the world as it is, and we are, to some degree, formed by it and tempted to live the lie: "How our will deviates in its inclination from that which is the will of God. He wants us to love truth; we love the lie. He wants us to desire the eternal; we, here below, lean toward what comes to an end. He wants us to desire sublime and great things; we, here below, desire base and earthly things" (W 42.4). The struggle, with God's help, to walk in the truth of humility, Teresa tells us, is "ointment for our wounds" (IC 3.2.6). In seeing the truth about ourselves, we can open ourselves to the healing power of the Divine Physician.

A RIGOROUS SELF-KNOWLEDGE

To walk in truth—to grow in the necessary virtue of humility—we must strive more and more to know ourselves. Just as Teresa is insistent about the need for humility, she is no less insistent on its essential connection to self-knowledge (W 39.5; IC 1.2.13, 6.5.10). Preparing for and entering ever more deeply into union with God therefore requires a constant, critical self-knowledge, a commitment to look squarely at ourselves as we are. In light of who God is, what we are meant to be, and the sad state of our lives in sin, we can never allow ourselves to lose our sense of our sin and our need.

Our capacity to deceive ourselves is often quite amazing, and our ability to accept uncritically the values and the norms of the world around us is immense. But as Teresa has warned us, so much of what society values can be merely superficial, or false, or even evil. By keeping our eyes fixed on Christ who is our truth and by allowing God to illuminate us to the truth in prayer, we can distinguish ever more clearly the truth and the lie in the world around us. And by a relentlessly self-critical gaze and by God revealing us to ourselves in prayer, we can confront what is false in us and ultimately allow God to uproot it completely.

Self-knowledge is especially important at the beginning of the journey, but Teresa is insistent that, in this life, we never pass beyond the need to reflect on ourselves before God. Self-knowledge is essential "even for those whom the Lord has brought into the very dwelling place where He abides" (IC 1.2.8). And it is necessary not just as a general attitude but as an understanding of oneself in every encounter in prayer: "And take care about this: however sublime the contemplation, let your prayer always begin and end with self-knowledge" (W 39.5).

In this life, we never transcend our need for self-knowledge and humility, though both come to function more by God's action and in light of God's grandeur:

> For humility, like the bee making honey in the beehive, is always at work. Without it, everything goes wrong. But let's remember that the bee doesn't fail to leave the beehive and fly about gathering nectar from the flowers. So it is with the soul in the room of self-knowledge; let it believe me and fly sometimes to ponder the grandeur and majesty of its God. Here it will discover its lowliness better than by thinking of itself. . . . And believe me, we shall practice much better virtue through God's help than by being tied down to our own misery. (IC 1.2.8)

We see again that for Teresa, our self-knowledge is always dependent on a knowledge of God. Without knowledge of God, we cannot have true knowledge of ourselves: "While we are on this earth nothing is more important to us than humility. . . . Let's strive to make more progress in self-knowledge. In my opinion we shall never completely know ourselves if we don't strive to know God. By gazing at His grandeur, we get in touch with our own lowliness; by looking at His purity, we shall see our own filth; by pondering His humility, we shall see how far we are from being humble" (IC 1.2.9).

WHAT HUMILITY IS NOT

Our discussion of Teresa's reflections on false honor, walking in truth, and self-knowledge has already provided a sense of her understanding of humility. Perhaps it might also be useful to look at what she says humility is not.

She warns her readers against "false humility," which can come in two forms or faces: a cowardice or timidity about aspiring to the great things to which God calls us or an inclination to a spirit of discouragement that is really a form of pride (L 7.1; IC 1.1.3). Both faces of false humility paralyze spiritual growth.[16]

By a relentlessly self-critical gaze and by God revealing us to ourselves in prayer, we can confront what is false in us and ultimately allow God to uproot it completely.

Teresa warns against a spiritual timidity that masks itself as true humility—those who, because they know they are sinners and utterly dependent on God, hold back from embracing God's invitation and the divine gifts to attain true union:

> Leave aside any of that faintheartedness that some persons have and think is humility. You see, humility doesn't consist

16. Málax, "Humilidad," 349–50; Castellano, "Espiritualidad teresiana," 254.

in refusing a favor the King offers you but in accepting such a favor and understanding how bountifully it comes to you and being delighted with it. What a nice kind of humility! I have the Emperor of heaven and earth in my house (for He comes to it in order to favor me and be happy with me), and out of humility I do not answer Him or stay with Him or take what He gives me, but I leave Him alone. Or, while He is telling me and begging me to ask Him for something, I do not do so but remain poor; and I even let Him go, for He sees that I never finish trying to make up my mind. Have nothing to do with this kind of humility. (W 28.3)

John of the Cross notes that the first invitations to contemplation are often quite subtle, and too many Christians miss them because they are not aware of them or know how to be attentive to them. Teresa is warning those who might ignore such invitations because they think themselves unworthy of such gifts. The simple fact is that they are indeed unworthy—and profoundly so—but that is not the point. The point is that in the divine mercy God is offering it, indeed sometimes "begging" us to ask and receive.

Acknowledging and accepting such divine gifts awakens love, because we are holding together both our unworthiness and amazement at God's gratuitous love. Teresa observes that we love others all the more when we recall what they do for us. The divine gifts are like precious jewels that, when we acknowledge and embrace them, fill us with gratitude and love (L 10.4–5). And in receiving these gifts, we are able to share our own gifts with others: "For how can people benefit and share their gifts lavishly if they do not understand that they are rich?" (L 10.6). False humility then is ultimately ungrateful, a hindrance to a deeper love for God, and an obstacle to the union to which God invites us.

In a similar way, false humility can take the form of discouragement and a temptation to give up the practice of prayer in the face of one's sins. Recognizing our sin, we think that we are not worthy to pray, that somehow God would not welcome our prayer. Teresa describes her own experience of this temptation early in *The Book of Her Life*: "This was the most terrible trick the devil could play on me, under the guise of humility: that seeing myself so corrupted I began to fear the practice of prayer" (L 7.1). But to give up prayer is not only a lack of true humility but it also only makes matters worse (L 19.4). This temptation may seem like a humble acknowledgment of the reality of sin, but really it is pride masking itself as humility. Discouragement because of our sinfulness shows that we are focused on ourselves. Perhaps we harbored some secret belief that we had already arrived at a more advanced spiritual state or that progress on the journey ultimately depended on our own efforts in the first place. "Now be also on guard, daughters, against some types of humility given by the devil in which great disquiet is felt about the gravity of our sins" (W 39.1).

In fact, it is true humility to acknowledge our sinfulness and never to lose sight of our need for God's help and mercy. It may seem then that there is a thin line between true and false humility in light of our sins. For Teresa, the clearest sign of the difference is that true humility "does not disturb or disquiet or agitate, however great it may be; it comes with peace, delight, and calm" (W 39.2; also L 25.13; L 30.9–10; L 31.16). She continues,

> Even though a person upon seeing himself so wretched understands clearly that he merits to be in hell, suffers affliction, thinks everyone should in justice abhor him, and almost doesn't dare ask for mercy, his pain, if the humility is genuine, comes with a sweetness in itself and a satisfaction that

it wouldn't want to be without. The pain of genuine humility doesn't agitate or afflict the soul; rather, this humility
expands it and enables it to serve God more. The other type
of pain disturbs everything, agitates everything, afflicts the
entire soul, and is very painful. I think the devil's aim is to
make us think we are humble and, in turn, if possible, make us
lose confidence in God. (W 39.2)

True humility then is not timidity, and it does not bring
discouragement. In fact, the reality is quite the contrary. Truly
humble persons know they must trust and abandon themselves
to God, and in their surrender to God's mercy they find courage and strength. Squarely recognizing their sin, they are nonetheless uplifted by the sure mercy and help of God. Authentic
humility brings with it a renewed dynamism to the Christian
life, based on what God can do in the humble soul. God "is a
friend of courageous souls if they walk in humility and without
trusting in self" (L 13.2).[17]

HUMILITY AND PRAYER

Because the personal truth, or identity, of the human is founded
in another—in God—it is only in relationship with the Other
that human persons can truly discover, conform themselves to,
and grow into the truth of human existence. We who are created
in the divine image can only know ourselves in relationship with
God. As we have said, according to Teresa's classic definition,
prayer is "nothing else than an intimate sharing between friends"
(L 8.5). It is in prayer then that human persons relate to God
who is the foundation of the truth about themselves. Prayer is
our access to God and to the truth about ourselves; therefore,

---

17. Málax, "Humilidad," 348; Herráiz, *Solo Dios Basta*, 260.

it is prayer that is essential to the humility by which we walk in the truth of our humanity before God.[18] As Teresa reminds us, the truest humility is ultimately God's gift to us, given in prayer: "Only humility can do something, a humility not acquired by the intellect, but by a clear perception that comprehends in a moment the truth that one would be unable to grasp in a long time through the work of the imagination about what a trifle we are and how very great God is" (W 32.13).

Prayer is the school of truth in which God reveals and infuses the divine Truth. It is in prayer that God gives light in order to understand the truth about God, about ourselves, and about reality around us. Perhaps this is nowhere more obvious than in the life of this Doctor of the Church who received profound understanding of divine truth not through formal theological training but through union with the source of all truth. In describing a key encounter with God, she tells us, "From this divine

> Truly humble persons know they must trust and abandon themselves to God, and in their surrender to God's mercy they find courage and strength.

Truth, which showed itself to me, there was engraved upon me, without my knowing how or what, a truth that gives me a new reverence for God. . . . Thus I understood that the Lord gave me understanding of what Truth itself is" (L 40.3). She continues in the next paragraph: "This truth, which I say was given to my understanding, is itself truth, and it is without beginning or end; all other truths depend upon this truth, just as all other

---

18. Herráiz, *Solo Dios Basta*, 252.

loves depend upon this love, and all other grandeurs on this grandeur" (L 40.4). In deep prayer, God gives a clearer vision of the truth, just as one who is taken from the ground to the top of a high watchtower would see the world around him or her in an entirely new way (see L 21.5).

Teresa has special warnings to give about a particular lack of humility that can be manifest in our life of prayer. For her, there is a particular lack of humility in desiring and especially in expecting consolations in prayer: "Oh, humility, humility! I don't know what kind of temptation I'm undergoing in this matter that I cannot help but think that anyone who makes such an issue of this dryness is a little lacking in humility" (IC 3.1.7). For Christians, however faithful and sincere, to desire and expect that God give them good feelings and affirmation in prayer or to expect God to give them the gift of contemplation is a lack of humility. It suggests a sense that someone can deserve something from God—and has a right to complain to God—if the expected reward is not given. Such a person would thereby manifest a forgetfulness of the truth about themselves before God. At another level, such attitudes would show that we are really, at some level, focused on self, on our own satisfaction and our own will, rather than wholly seeking God. This lack of humility in regard to dryness in prayer reveals that often "we are fonder of consolations than we are of the cross" (IC 3.1.9).

Authentic prayer depends on humility and is linked with patience—waiting on God. In her classic treatise on prayer imaged as four ways of watering a garden, Teresa notes that dryness in prayer can be "an authentic weeding and pulling up of the remaining bad growth by its roots" by which God prepares us for deeper, more passive prayer (L 14.9).[19] God

---

19. Málax, "Humilidad," 347; Herráiz, *Solo Dios Basta*, 251–52.

chooses the way and the timing for each individual, and anyone who is walking in the truth is content to wait on the divine will and pleasure (IC 6.9.15). Without growth in humility, there can be no growth in prayer: "Since this edifice is built entirely on humility, the closer one comes to God the more progress there must be in this virtue; and if there is no progress in humility, everything is going to be ruined" (L 12.4; also L 22.11). Whether in the matter of dryness or the reception of contemplative gifts, humility is always the appropriate stance of any authentic prayer: "Let them consider how true humility consists very much in great readiness to be content with whatever the Lord may want to do with them" (W 17.6).

DIVINE MODELS OF HUMILITY

Humility, for Teresa, is first of all an attribute of God. This is a distinct and lovely insight: God is first in humility. Our all-good God humbly reaches out to sinners, and the divine humility is evident in the incarnation of the Son in human flesh and his innocent suffering and death on the cross for sinners (W 33.2, 5). Now, God demonstrates further humility by coming to us in prayer to teach us (W 26.1) and even more marvelously in taking us to be a spouse in spiritual betrothal and the mystical marriage, which are Teresa's images for the deepest experience of spiritual union with God (IC 5.4.3). In fact, she says, God "never tires in humiliating himself for us" (F 3.13).

By attending to the divine example, to the example of Christ and of the Blessed Virgin Mary (W 13.3; M 6.7), and the saints (IC 1.2.11), we will learn the path of true humility. By it, we will enter into true communion with God. Drawing on the image of playing chess, Teresa tells us that our humility is like the queen in the chess game, and with it we will make the King surrender;

God will be "checkmated" by our humility. It was the Blessed Virgin's humility, Teresa tells us, that drew the King from heaven into Mary's womb, and with the same virtue we too will draw God to our souls. "And realize that the one who has more humility will be the one who possesses Him more; and the one who has less will possess Him less" (W 16.2).

HUMILITY AND TRANSFORMATION

For Teresa of Avila, humility is situated in the tension between our inherent dignity and the fact of our sin, between our misery and God's mercy, between our need and God's gratuitous giving. Before God, humility is the attitude of one who knows that everything depends on God and all good proceeds from the divine hand. Before other persons, humility is the capacity to live without pretensions, without seeking after superficial and false support, with a willingness to accept the last place. In the face of one's own sin and need, humility is the doorway through which we can allow God to forgive, to heal, and to move us forward (IC 3.2.6).[20]

Humility is ultimately freeing. It frees us to surrender to God's action. It frees us from being burdened by excessive self-concern, from feeling the need to defend ourselves, from concern about what other people think of us (W 15). Knowing the truth of our own dignity, we can see the true dignity of others. Recognizing our own sinfulness, we are able to see beyond the faults of others to see their goodness. Seeing ourselves as we are and free from the need to compete with others, we are free to truly love others and to rejoice when they are praised (IC 5.3.11).[21]

---

20. Castellano, "Espiritualidad teresiana," 254.

21. Herráiz, *Solo Dios Basta*, 257–59.

Humility is central to Teresa's spiritual teaching. When we understand it in the context of her time and her thought, we can see why she considered it to be at the heart of the essential foundation for contemplation. The word "humility" (in Spanish, *humildad*) comes from a Latin root that refers to "earth" or "ground." To be humble is to be like the earth. In Teresa's wonderful image of the stages of prayer as different ways of watering a garden (L 11–22), she invites us to think of our souls as gardens to be tended. To be humble means to be like fertile earth, receptive to receive the water that God will send in abundance. The highest degree of prayer involves no work on our part. God simply rains the gift of the divine self on fertile and humble soil.

7

MUY DETERMINADA DETERMINACIÓN
(A VERY DETERMINED DETERMINATION)

They must have a great and very resolute determination
[muy determinada determinación] to persevere until
reaching the end, come what may, happen what may,
whatever work is involved, whatever criticism arises,
whether they arrive or whether they die on the road or
even if they don't have courage for the trials that are met,
or if the whole world collapses. (W 21.2)

For Teresa of Jesus, a "very determined determination" is
an utterly essential element for growth in prayer and for
the spiritual journey more generally. It is at the heart or
the backbone of the liberating effort that this journey requires.[1]
Any journey to arrive at a distant but worthy destination, after
all, often involves its ups and downs, its steep climbs and low val-
leys, possible distractions, obstacles, wrong turns, and mishaps.
Every worthwhile earthly journey then requires a firm spirit of
determination to reach the desired end for which we set out. As
Teresa says of the spiritual journey, "A great treasure is gained by
traveling this road; no wonder we have to pay what seems like a
high price" (W 21.1).

---

1. Tomás Alvarez, *Comentarios a las obras de Santa Teresa: Libro de la vida, Camino de perfección, Castillo interior* (Burgos, Spain: Editorial Monte Carmelo, 2005), 302; Tomás Alvarez,
"Determiné," in *Estudios teresianos III: Doctrina espiritual* (Burgos, Spain: Editorial Monte Carmelo, 1996), 513.

In the same way, if we are to progress steadily from the outer dwelling places of the interior castle to the most interior—if we are to pass from sinful separation from God to intimate union with God—then we must set out and progress in this very great and resolute determination. The daily, progressive practice of prayer, love of others, detachment, and humility depend on maintaining and strengthening such resolve. In this sense, although Teresa speaks of three essential virtues, determination can rightly be called the fourth necessary virtue.[2] Its importance is evident from the fact that the word or a form of it appears almost 160 times in *The Book of Her Life*, *The Way of Perfection*, and *The Interior Castle*.[3]

A Very Determined Woman

Teresa of Avila herself was a woman of very great determination. Although she recounts the various youthful vacillations that plagued her early religious life at the Monastery of the Incarnation before her deeper conversion (see, for example, L 6.4; 7.19; 9.7),[4] even in the midst of describing that period in her life, she demonstrates a deeper characteristic of inner resolve.[5] Reading

---

2. Alvarez, *Comentarios*, 302, 402.

3. The various forms of the Spanish word for determination are often appropriately translated into English as "resolve" or "resolution" as well as "determination." Tomás Alvarez observes that some form of the word "determination" appears fifty-two times in *The Way of Perfection* in the following forms: *determinar/se*, twenty-six times; *determinación*, twenty-three times; *determinadamente*, two times; and *determinacioncilla*, one time. Some form of the word appears seventy-seven times in *The Book of Her Life* and twenty-six times in *The Interior Castle* (Alvarez, "Determiné," 511; see also Secundino Castro, *Ser Cristiano según Santa Teresa: Teología y espiritualidad*, 2nd ed. [Madrid: Editorial de Espiritualidad, 1985], 309n19).

4. Félix Málax,"Determinación," in *Diccionario de Santa Teresa*, ed. Tomás Alvarez, 2nd ed. (Burgos, Spain: Editorial Monte Carmelo, 2006), 217.

5. Alvarez identifies numerous instances of expressions of determination in Teresa's early life (many translated again into English as "resolved" or "decided") in the following passages from *The Book of Her Life*: L 3.4, 3.5, 4 (title), 4.3, 13.7, 26.3, 35.6 (Alvarez, "Determiné," 508–10).

the account of her entrance into the Incarnation in the fourth chapter of her *Life*, we find a particularly good example of this capacity for determined action. Leaving her beloved, widowed father required, she says, the greatest resolve along with God's help or she would have lacked the courage to proceed. In fact, she entered more because of reasoned resolve to find the best path to accomplishing God's will and attaining eternal life than because of a clear and firm desire to be a nun. God, she concluded, "favors those who use force with themselves to serve Him" (L 4.2). This perhaps sounds a bit grim. However, within an hour of entering the monastery, she says, she was filled with great happiness.

In the end, it is simply impossible to conceive that a cloistered nun in sixteenth-century Spain could have accomplished what Teresa did through her foundations and writings without such firm determination. She was, after all, a woman without formal theological training, in a culture that did not have a particularly high opinion of women, and in an age that lived under the vigilant gaze of the Inquisition. No doubt Teresa herself would have attributed everything that she accomplished to God working through her, and, of course, that would be true. All virtue is the result of grace at work in us. At the same time, in Teresa, God seems to have chosen a human instrument with an innate, characteristic spirit of resolve.

Church historian J. Mary Luti ties Teresa's spirit of determination, in a particular way, to her struggle to discern the origins—divine, merely human, or diabolical—of her first experiences of mystical graces.[6] As Teresa describes in the twenty-fifth chapter of the *Life*, her first confessors and advisers, learned

---

6. J. Mary Luti, *Teresa of Avila's Way*, Way of the Christian Mystics 13 (Collegeville, Minn.: Michael Glazier/Liturgical Press, 1991), 61–65.

and sincere in her eyes, were quick and adamant in suggesting that the devil was at work in her experiences. They cautioned her to be concerned for the inquiring gaze of the Inquisition, which was hyper-vigilant in its hunt for false mystics, especially among women. All the same, Teresa, while recognizing that she was lacking in theological training in comparison to the academic learning of her guides, could not overcome her profound sense that her experiences were from God. In the midst of this anguished struggle, she heard the words of God: "Do not fear, daughter, for I am, and I will not abandon you; do not fear" (L 25.18). She immediately felt "fortitude, courage, security, quietude, and light." She concludes, "His words are works!" She had learned the importance of a determination that was firmly grounded in trust in the One who gives courage and whose very word is effective.

Teresa begins *The Way of Perfection* by describing the rationale for the Carmelite reform. She reports that, as she looked out on the troubles of the church, it seemed to her that God had "so many enemies and so few friends." And so, while recognizing her own limitations, she resolved (*determiné*) to do what was in her power and to urge her nuns to do the same, with the same determination (W 1.2). And this "I resolved" of the first chapter of the *Way* is a key to the spiritual doctrine that would follow. Determination, for Teresa, is not merely a personality characteristic with which some individuals seem endowed. It is instead a decision and attitude that must be chosen and nurtured in anyone who wants to advance in prayer and in the journey to union with God.[7]

---

7. Alvarez, "Determiné," 505.

THE MEANING OF THE DETERMINATION

"Resolutions were meant to be broken." This is a popular adage in our day that we often hear around New Year's Day, or more probably, not too long thereafter. We make many resolutions that we know we will never keep. In the end, such resolutions are more like wishes, hopes, ideals, or perhaps just fantasies. We make them without even believing for ourselves that they are attainable. When Teresa of Avila speaks of resolute determination or resolution, she means nothing like that. In her mind, resolutions are *not* meant to be broken. They are *never* meant to be broken.

Determination is grounded in a fundamental and unswerving choice for God— a fundamental and radical choice for God that admits no half measures or vacillations, whatever may come.

When Teresa speaks of determination, she means a deep, firm, abiding commitment—something that is most definitely not occasional, passing, or superficial. Determination is grounded in a fundamental and unswerving choice for God—a fundamental and radical choice for God that admits no half measures or vacillations, whatever may come. As Jesus says in the Gospel, we must not put our hand to the plow and then look back (Lk 9:62), or as St. Paul tells us, we must be like runners who must run to finish the race without allowing ourselves to be distracted along the way (1 Cor 9:24–27).

We must love God in return for the divine love, and we must do so with firm resolve: "And this love, daughters, must not be fabricated in our imaginations but proved by deeds. And don't think that He needs our works; He needs the determination of our wills" (IC 3.1.7). In the end, we cannot fully receive the divine self-giving unless and until we have given ourselves completely—which cannot be done without a firm resolve in the process: "The whole point is that we should give ourselves to Him with complete determination. . . . He takes what we give Him; but He doesn't give Himself completely until we give ourselves completely" (W 28.12).[8]

THE DETERMINATION TO PRAY

At the heart of Teresa's conception of determination as a fundamental attitude on the way of transformation is the resolve never to turn back on the path of prayer. She summarizes this clearly in the title of chapter 23 of *The Way of Perfection*: "Treats of how important it is for one who has begun the path of prayer not to turn back and speaks once more of the great value that lies in beginning with determination" (W 23). She urges us never to give up but rather to give time to prayer each day whatever may come, regardless of the state of our soul, or however we personally experience the prayer. Recalling the spiritual inconstancy of her early life as a nun, she reflects gratefully that she had the grace and determination never to leave aside her prayer: "I see clearly the great mercy the Lord bestowed on me; for though I continued to associate with the world, I had the courage to practice prayer. I say courage, for I do not know what would require greater courage among all the things there are in the world than to betray the king and know that he knows it and yet never leave

8. Jesús Castellano, "Espiritualidad teresiana: Experiencia y doctrina," in *Introducción a la lectura de Santa Teresa*, ed. Alberto Barrientos (Madrid: Editorial de Espiritualidad, 2002), 255–57; Málax, "Determinación," 217.

his presence" (L 8.2).[9] To those who struggle with prayer, are tempted to give up, or feel unworthy at times because of sin, she says emphatically, "If the soul perseveres in prayer, in the midst of sins, temptations, and failures of a thousand kinds that the devil places in its path, in the end, I hold as certain, the Lord will draw it forth to the harbor of salvation as—now it seems—He did for me" (L 8.4; see also L 8.5). And for those with tendencies to scruples, Teresa assures us elsewhere that God "doesn't look at trifles as much as you think" (W 41.8).

Teresa, the mystic and great teacher of prayer, was herself no stranger to the temptation to give up on prayer as a result of the experience of dryness in prayer. For all of us, it is easy to feel that "nothing is happening" or we are "wasting our time" when our efforts at prayer are met with aridity. Teresa's account of her experience in this regard is so rich that it bears a lengthier quote:

> And very often, for some years, I was more anxious that the hour I had determined to spend in prayer be over than I was to remain there, and more anxious to listen for the striking of the clock than to attend to other good things. And I don't know what heavy penance could have come to mind that frequently I would not have gladly undertaken rather than recollect myself in the practice of prayer. It is certain that so unbearable was the force used by the devil, or coming from my wretched habits, to prevent me from going to prayer, and

---

9. In the previous chapter of *The Book of Her Life*, Teresa had described how she had previously given up the practice of prayer for more than a year because of a misguided sense of unworthiness (L 7.11). But her father's good example of prayer, his holy manner of dying, and the counsel of her deceased father's confessor led her to take up prayer again with a firm resolve never to give it up again. Her own experience of this misguided and ultimately false sense of humility became the source of her insistence that people must never give up on the practice of prayer even if they feel unworthy.

so unbearable the sadness I felt on entering the oratory, that I had to muster up all my courage (and they say that I have no small amount of that, and it is observed that God has given me more than women usually have, but I have made poor use of it) in order to force myself; and in the end the Lord helped me. (L 8.7)

Teresa has expressed her experience dramatically, but it probably rings true to everyone who has tried to build up a real practice of prayer. But her response to the temptation to give up on prayer is precisely a very determined determination!

With prayer, we must simply begin and be determined to persevere: "Whoever has not begun the practice of prayer, I beg for the love of the Lord not to go without so great a good. . . . And if one perseveres, I trust then in the mercy of God, who never fails to repay anyone who has taken Him for a friend" (L 8.5). And then she continues with her classic definition of prayer: "For mental prayer in my opinion is nothing else than an intimate sharing between friends; it means taking time frequently to be alone with Him who we know loves us" (L 8.5). Perseverance in prayer then is not simply a matter of stern self-discipline. It requires a constant reminder to ourselves that prayer is communion with a friend who loves us. This is evident in the first sentences of the treatise on prayer that begins with chapter 11 of *The Book of Her Life*: "Well, let us speak now of those who are beginning to be servants of love. This doesn't seem to me to mean anything else than to follow resolutely [*determinarnos a seguir*] by means of this path of prayer Him who has loved us so much" (L 11.1). For Teresa, prayer, determination, God's love, and our responding love are intimately interwoven.

REASONS FOR BEING DETERMINED

Teresian scholar Tomás Alvarez identifies three reasons why Teresa tells us we must begin and proceed with a firm determination.[10] The first reason for this firm resolve is that we are giving our very selves in response to the gift of divine love. And we are *giving*—not merely *lending* with the possibility of taking back what we have given. As Teresa says, in the end, we are giving so little in comparison to what God is giving, it would be petty indeed to give something so relatively small as ourselves with the expectation of holding back or asking for a return (W 23.1). God has given, offered, and promised so much that we simply must be firmly resolved to give in return, regardless of the difficulty this self-giving entails. Determination to progress in self-giving is grounded in a grateful recognition of the divine self-giving to us.

The second reason for determination is that it discourages the devil. A person who begins with a strong resolve to succeed or arrive is less vulnerable to the devil's wiles. In other words, the more determined we are, the less susceptible we are to temptation. If, on the other hand, our resolution is weak or our determination halfhearted from the very beginning, we will actually find ourselves all the more tempted. Think again of New Year's resolutions: if we begin halfheartedly or without a firm sense that we can actually succeed, we will be ill equipped to face the inevitable temptations to give up. The devil, as Teresa puts it, is "extremely afraid of determined souls" (W 23.4). On the journey to the inmost chamber of the interior castle, the person must not waver: "Let the soul always heed the warning not to be conquered. If the devil sees that it has the strong determination to

---

10. Alvarez, *Comentarios*, 405–6.

lose its life and repose and all that he offers it rather than return to the first room [of the interior castle], he will abandon it much more quickly" (IC 2.1.6).

The third reason for determination, according to Teresa, is that it yields the ability to struggle more valiantly. If we begin with the commitment not to fail—and hold on to that resolve—we will surely win the battles that lie ahead (W 23.5). Here, the emphasis is not so much the ability to resist temptation but rather the strength more positively to struggle in order to accomplish great things. We will look below at Teresa's battle images in relation to the virtues of determination and fortitude.

ESPECIALLY AT THE BEGINNING

A very resolute determination is essential at every stage of the spiritual journey. We must never give up or vacillate. Still, beginning with a firm resolve and growing in that initial determination is especially important. Teresa's entire focus in the discussion of the second dwelling places (of seven) in *The Interior Castle* is the need to begin with determination. The title of the only chapter devoted to these second dwellings begins, "Discusses the importance of perseverance if one is to reach the final dwellings places" (IC 2.1). In the first and outermost of the dwellings, the person had done little more than step inside the door of the interior castle. That step is no small accomplishment, but the temptations to go back out to the sinful and superficial world outside the castle remain strong. Having stepped in and begun, the person must be encouraged to make a firm resolve and move forward with a very determined determination. "These first acts of determination are very important," she teaches (L 13.3).

The first half of *The Way of Perfection*, as we have seen, focuses on the three essential virtues that are the necessary foundation for prayer. Having then begun the discussion of prayer in chapter 19, she titles chapter 21, "Tells how important it is to begin the practice of prayer with great determination and not pay any attention to obstacles set up by the devil" (W 21). Then, after a chapter explaining the meaning of mental prayer, she returns to the importance of determination, as we see in the title of chapter 23: "Treats of how important it is for one who has begun the path of prayer not to turn back and speaks once more of the great value that lies in beginning with determination" (W 23). Teresa believes that she cannot speak seriously about prayer without emphasizing again and again that we must begin and persevere with a very firm resolve.

In fact, it is important to begin with determination, even if one should falter or fall, frequently or occasionally. Teresa points encouragingly to the example of St. Peter who stepped out of the boat in a howling storm at sea to walk on the water to Jesus (Mt 14:22–33). It is true that he faltered and began to sink, but the point is that he started out with determination: "I often thought that St. Peter didn't lose anything when he threw himself into the sea, even though he grew frightened afterward. These first acts of determination are very important" (L 13.3). Missing our prayer on occasion, becoming slack for a time, or falling into sin is no reason to give up. We must begin with a prudent determination about what we can do with God's help. If we fail or fall, we must pick ourselves up and set out again, renewing the resolve with which we began.

It is especially critical for the beginner in prayer to set out with a determination not to be distracted by the desire for good feelings in prayer, nor to be discouraged by the absence of such spiritual consolations: "It is an important matter for beginners in prayer to start off by becoming detached from every kind of satisfaction and to enter the path solely with the determination to help Christ carry the cross like good cavaliers, who desire to serve their king at no salary since their salary is certain" (L 15.11). To be able to persevere in prayer without concern for the presence or absence of consolation is a sign of authentic progress along the way: "It should be carefully noted . . . that the soul that begins to walk along this path of mental prayer with determination and that can succeed in paying little attention to whether this delight and tenderness is lacking or whether the Lord gives it (or to whether it has much consolation or no consolation) has traveled a great part of the way" (L 11.13). As Teresa says in relation to becoming detached from family, the key is to remember that everything worthwhile is found in seeking Jesus with a firm resolve: "What helps is that the soul embrace the good Jesus our Lord with determination, for since in Him everything is found, in Him everything is forgotten" (W 9.5). The goal is growth in authentic, prayerful communion with Jesus himself—not the maintenance of good feelings in prayer that may or may not be a sign of the divine presence.

For Teresa, determination finds its greatest example and truest justification in the example of Jesus in his crucifixion. We must embrace the cross, she insists, from the very beginning and be prepared to carry it to the end: "For there are many who begin, yet never reach the end. I believe this is due mainly to a failure to embrace the cross from the beginning" (L 11.15). We must begin and continue with a clear expectation that the path of deepening prayer and transformation will involve dryness and even hardship. To set out without this clear-eyed vision is to invite the speedy onset of discouragement and even failure. Jesus, she reminds us, tells us to take up our cross and follow him, and in this, he gives us the example and leads the way. We must resolutely do so from the very beginning (L 15.13). Determination, then, is a daily carrying of the cross that is fortified by the aspiration to arrive where the Lord has gone before us, through and ultimately beyond the current experience of hardship, patience, and disciplined perseverance.[11] As she bluntly tells her nuns: "Be determined, Sisters, that you came to die for Christ, not to live comfortably for Christ" (W 10.5).

> To be able to persevere in prayer without concern for the presence or absence of consolation is a sign of authentic progress along the way.

But, for all of her insistence on firm determination, Teresa does not want us to be grim, our brows furrowed with intense resolve. Rather, she wants her nuns (and us) to be "affable and understanding in such a way that everyone you talk to will love your conversation and desire your manner of living and acting, and not be frightened and intimidated by virtue" (W 41.7). In fact, she adds that one sign of authentic holiness is that it makes us more sociable.

DETERMINATION AND FORTITUDE

Avila, the place in which Teresa was born and spent the first fifty years of her life, was (and is) a magnificently walled city. It possessed a rich and proud military history. The Monastery of the Incarnation has a grand view of those medieval battlements. In the sixteenth century, Spain was constantly at war to expand and protect its empire. In fact, several of Teresa's brothers fought in the growing Spanish empire in the New World. It is therefore

---

11. Castellano, "Espiritualidad teresiana," 256–57.

perhaps no surprise that Teresa often describes determination in military terms: castle, fight, battle, soldiers, captains, standard-bearers, conquest, and even the strategies of the game of chess.[12] Along the way, she tells her nuns that they must be strong and be prepared to "fight even to the death in the search, for you are not here for any other reason than to fight. You must always proceed with this determination to die rather than fail to reach the end of the journey" (W 20.2). We must be like soldiers who are always eager to fight without fear of the enemy and with an eye fixed on the treasures that come with victory (W 38.1–2). We must fight with the determination of soldiers who know the importance of the victory to be won and of the riches to be gained—spurred on by the knowledge that the enemy will not spare their lives if they surrender or are defeated (W 23.5).

As the use of military and battle images suggests, determination is linked with fortitude or courage: "Indeed a great mercy does He bestow on anyone to whom He gives the grace and courage to resolve [*determinarse*] to strive for this great good with every ounce of energy. For God does not deny Himself to anyone who perseveres. Little by little He will measure out the courage sufficient to attain this victory" (L 11.4).

Here it might be useful to say a few words about how St. Thomas Aquinas speaks of the virtue of fortitude—not, of course, because Teresa studied the works of Aquinas (though she consulted many learned Dominicans) but because his reflection may shed further light on what Teresa means by determination.[13] There is no reason to doubt that Teresa would have heard aspects of the Scholastic discussion of virtues from her confessors and guides, many of them Dominicans, even if

---

12. Alvarez, "Determiné," 510–11.

13. Alvarez, *Comentarios*, 302.

personally she never undertook the formal study of theology or philosophy.

For Aquinas, the virtue of fortitude or courage is the habitual disposition—the abiding tendency or the consistent character trait—to overcome obstacles to attain the good (*Summa Theologiae* II–IIae, q. 123). As Teresa's use of military images suggests, the courage of soldiers in battle is a particularly clear instance of the virtue of fortitude. But fortitude is also essential for more mundane challenges in more ordinary circumstances. This virtue is necessary to confront and overcome, with consistency and without great inner struggle, whatever difficulty, challenge, or danger stands between us and a good that we want to obtain.

As Teresa says of determination, the virtue of fortitude begins with a decision to embrace a fundamental attitude, but then it requires sustained effort to develop it. As with all of the moral virtues, the virtue of courage is built up over time by the choices we make—confronting head on, in a consistent way, one choice after another, regardless of the challenge, great or small, that stands between us and our goal. With eyes of faith, of course, we see that both fortitude and determination depend, more deeply, on the action of God in grace. Without divine assistance, we are not capable on our own of doing any good.[14] On the other hand, Teresa is certain that God "is a friend of courageous souls if they walk in humility without trusting in self" (L 13.2).

---

14. We will not pursue here St. Thomas's discussion of *infused* moral virtues (as distinct from the virtues that we acquire by own efforts) that, more properly speaking, direct our efforts to union with God, nor his reflection on fortitude as one of the seven gifts of the Holy Spirit. In fact, those topics would likely shed further light on what Teresa is saying about determination, but our purpose here is not to offer a full comparison of Teresa and Aquinas or of the mutual light they might each shed on the writings of the other.

Aquinas suggests that closely related to the virtue of fortitude are four allied virtues that he calls magnanimity (*Summa Theologiae* II–IIae, q. 129), magnificence (q. 134), patience (q. 136), and perseverance (q. 137). In our day, we probably don't think of the first two, magnanimity and magnificence, as virtues or perhaps even as dispositions that people can or should possess. For our purposes here, we can think of them together as a greatness of spirit or an abiding disposition to aspire to great things. Fortitude, as a stable attitude and disposition, is aided by these abiding attitudes to face what we must in order to arrive at noble goals. Teresa herself is a particularly superb example of an ability to aspire to great things: at an earthly level, in regard to her project of establishing the reform of the Carmelites; and at a more spiritual level, in regard to the contemplation and union to which she so earnestly and resolutely aspired. Our determination, she suggests, is made possible by holding in our consciousness the wonder of what God wants to give to us. "I marvel," she says, "how important it is to be courageous in striving for great things along this path" (L 13.2). And it was to just such greatness of aspiration that she called her nuns (and us!)—soldiers, as she says, who fight bravely because they know the importance of the victory and the treasure to be won. Even while insisting on dogged perseverance, Teresa urges hers nuns to set their goals high: "Keep in mind that I say we should all try to be contemplatives, since we are not here for any other reason. And we should try not just for a year, nor only for two, nor even for just ten" (W 18.3; see also W 20.2).

For St. Thomas, the third virtue related to fortitude, the virtue of patience, is the abiding tendency to endure or bear evils inflicted by others. This is a more passive or docile face of courage, though inasmuch as it is authentically the virtue of patience and not merely passive acquiescence, it too requires the inner strength entailed in fortitude. It is clear that for Teresa patience is essential both to loving others in community and to humility. This is as true today for all of us as it was for her and her nuns. While love involves active service of others, it also includes bearing with those around us, whether in a family, in the workplace, or in community living. Humility too requires the patience to accept what may seem to be little offenses, slights, or injustices from others. The determination that must be partnered with love and humility includes this element of patience. Teresa speaks in a particular way about the need to wait patiently in times of dry prayer. In one of her lovely, homey images, she compares our efforts at prayer to the gardener who waters the garden without apparent result, waiting for the flowers to bloom. This is, she assures us, God's hidden weeding of our garden by which God is teaching us to wait humbly. In fact, the divine gardener can nourish the garden without water. The flowers will yet bloom for those who can wait (see L 14.9).

> The divine gardener can nourish the garden without water. The flowers will yet bloom for those who can wait!

Perseverance, the fourth of the virtues related to fortitude, is the abiding ability to hold firm, to stay the course, to wait actively to obtain a good that can be a long time in coming or in attaining. As we have seen, for Teresa, determination clearly involves the more active aspect of fortitude or courage: facing head on anything that stands between us and union with God. But just as clearly and essentially, it involves a spirit of perseverance, whether in prayer or in the practice of the three essential virtues.

OUR DETERMINATION DEPENDS ON GOD

With all of Teresa's insistence on the utter necessity of a resolute determination, it might appear that her goal is the attainment of some sort of spiritual heroism built on our own effort.
But Teresa of Avila is supremely aware of our human weakness.
As much as she insists on our effort to remain determined in
the practice of prayer and in living the essential virtues, she is
equally insistent that this determination must come from and
be sustained by God (ST 3.10; L 22.15; W 18.2; IC 7.4.10).[15]
As we noted above, this truth became clear to her when God
calmed her anxieties about her first mystical graces and empowered her to confront her doubting spiritual guides. This is true
for all of us, whether it is the initial good resolve of beginners or
the extraordinary courage of the martyrs: "I see clearly that the
martyrs did nothing of themselves in suffering torments, for the
soul well knows that fortitude comes from another" (L 16.4).
It is God who empowers us to begin with determination, and it
is God who enables us to persevere to the end: "Indeed a great
mercy does He bestow on anyone to whom He gives the grace
and courage to resolve [*determinarse*] to strive for this good with
every ounce of energy. For God does not deny Himself to anyone who perseveres. Little by little He will measure out the courage sufficient to attain this victory" (L 11.4).

Our determination then grows in proportion to our
ability to be open and surrendered to God: "When we are
more determined we are less confident of ourselves, for confidence must be placed in God" (W 41.4).[16] Our determination is therefore paradoxically rooted in the recognition and

---

15. Málax, "Determinación," 220; Castro, *Ser Cristiano*, 311.

16. Alvarez, "Determiné," 512.

acceptance of our weakness. In this, Teresa reflects the experience of St. Paul: "Whenever I am weak, then I am strong" (2 Cor 12:10). Any authentic human resolve must be grounded in trust in God's fidelity and in the divine determination to bring us into union (W 23.5). Our determination is rooted in God's determination.

Our failure to attain union with God in this life and to do great works is not because God's help is lacking. The fault is our own lack of the necessary resolve: "O greatness of God! How you manifest Your power in giving courage to an ant! How true, my Lord, that it is not because of You that those who love You fail to do great works but because of our own cowardice and pusillanimity. Since we are never determined, but full of human prudence and a thousand fears, You, consequently, my God, do not do Your marvelous and great works" (F 2.7). Having mentioned Aquinas's discussion of the virtue of fortitude and its related virtues, it might be worth noting that he lists cowardliness (*Summa Theologiae* II–IIae, q. 125), pusillanimity or faintheartedness (q. 133), and smallness of spirit (q.135) as vices contrary to fortitude and its related virtues. Cowardice, timidity, and restricted aspirations are the opposite of Teresian determination.

Even exalted and extraordinary mystical graces and encounters themselves, says Teresa, are given in order to provide us greater strength to persevere—more than merely to give us spiritual delight: "Thus I hold for certain that these favors are meant to fortify our weakness . . . that we may be able to imitate Him in His great sufferings" (IC 7.4.4).[17] At the same time, such mystical graces and extraordinary experiences themselves require a special courage given by God in order to accept and embrace them. Teresa often describes her initial fear in receiving

---

17. Castro, *Ser Cristiano*, 310.

a new mystical gift. To bear the inflow of the transcendent God requires a divinely given courage.[18]

Setting out with a strong resolve, we must be careful that our determination is not to follow along a path of our own choosing, no matter how sincere and good. Rather, we must set out resolutely along the path that God wills for us. We must be determined to do God's will and not our own: "Believe me, the safest way is to want only what God wants. He knows more than we ourselves do, and He loves us. Let us place ourselves in His hands so that His will may be done in us, and we cannot err if with a determined will we always maintain this attitude" (IC 6.9.16).[19] We must always ask God to give us the strength precisely to do the divine will, whatever it is. In a beautiful passage that sings of Teresa's utter resolve to do God will, she prays:

> Your will, Lord, be done in me in every way and manner that You, my Lord, want. If You want it to be done with trials, strengthen me and let them come; if with persecutions, illnesses, dishonors, and a lack of life's necessities, here I am; I will not turn away, my Father, nor is it right that I turn my back on You. Since Your Son gave You this will of mine in the name of all, there's no reason for any lack on my part. But grant me the favor of Your kingdom that I may do Your will, since He asked for this kingdom for me, and use me as You would Your own possession, in conformity with Your will. (W 32.10)

---

18. Kavanaugh provides numerous citations to illustrate this divine gift of courage. Kieran Kavanaugh and Carol Lisi, *The Interior Castle*, study ed. (Washington, D.C.: ICS Publications, 2010), 262n269.

19. Málax, "Determinación," 220.

8

⋯⋰⋰⋯

TRANSFORMED BY PRAYER

The Book of Her Life is sometimes called St. Teresa's autobiography. More accurately, it is the story of the unfolding of her friendship with God and of her spiritual experiences placed in a narrative framework. In chapter 9, she describes her "conversion" to a deeper life of prayer, provoked by a chance encounter with an image of the wounded Christ and the reading of St. Augustine's *Confessions*. In chapter 10, she begins to speak of contemplative prayer and her mystical experiences. Then, in chapters 11 through 22, she offers a treatise on prayer, using the image of the four ways to water a garden in order to describe deepening degrees of prayer. This teaching might at first seem like a long, albeit valuable, digression. In fact, it lays the foundation for Teresa's descriptions of the yet deeper mystical experiences that will follow.

When Teresa returns to the more narrative structure of the *Life* in chapter 23, she writes, "This is another, new book from here on—I mean another, new life. The life dealt with up to this point was mine; the one I lived from the point where I began to explain these things about prayer is the one God lived in me— according to the way it appears to me—because I think it would have been impossible in so short a time to get rid of so many bad habits and deeds. May the Lord be praised who freed me from myself" (L 23.1). Teresa is telling us that through contemplative prayer and the deeper mystical gifts, God has effected a transformation within her. In the fifth dwelling places of *The Interior Castle*, she will use the image of a silkworm transformed into a butterfly to describe this change. (We will examine this metaphor in some detail in the conclusion since, through it, Teresa offers an overarching image for this way of transformation.) To arrive at this point, she says, one needs to have worked with great care to practice those virtues that are "very, very much" needed (IC 5.1.1). But now, increasingly, the work and the transformation is the result of God's gracious work.

Another image that Teresa uses for this transformation in both the *Life* and in *The Interior Castle*, though unfolded with far less detail, is the mythical phoenix that "after it is burned rises again from the same ashes, so afterward the soul becomes another, with different desires and great fortitude. It doesn't seem to be what it was before, but begins to walk on the Lord's path with new purity" (L 39.23; see also IC 6.4.3). This image includes the element of a divine fire that consumes the old self with its sins and faults and yields a new self risen from the old. Through these encounters with God, the person is left "with such freedom and dominion over all things that it doesn't know itself" (L 20.23).

VIRTUES AS THE FRUIT OF PRAYER

When God gives the gift of contemplation and the deepening experience of divine union, the virtues now become the fruit of God's work that we embrace. Previously, Teresa had envisaged the person of prayer as the gardener of the soul who worked to prepare the soil and make it fertile for the gift of contemplation. But with the reception and unfolding of that gift, "the Lord so desires to help the gardener here that He Himself becomes practically the gardener and the one who does everything" (L 16.1; see also L 17.1). It is God who now does the work so that we can grow further in virtue (L 21.10).

The fact that virtue is the fruit of contemplative prayer and union is grounded in the reality that what God is giving is not something separate from the divine self. God is not just providing help to the person from "outside." Rather, by uniting the person with the divine ever more deeply, God is becoming increasingly the principal agent of the person's acting and being. The Lord told Teresa one day after she had received Communion, "It [the soul] detaches itself from everything, daughter, so as to abide more with me. It is no longer the soul that lives but I" (L 18.14). The person is drawing ever closer to "the true Virtue, which is God, from whence come all the virtues" (L 14.5).

> By uniting the person with the divine ever more deeply, God is becoming increasingly the principal agent of the person's acting and being.

In the later part of the treatise on prayer in *The Book of Her Life* in which Teresa describes these profound experiences, she also details their effects, noting that the person gives to God "the key of its will" and becomes obsessed with serving God (L 20.22, 21.5). Those so blessed discover a new freedom and self-dominion (L 20.23, 25). They see more lucidly that all merely human honor and reputation is the "lie" (L 20.26), and they laugh at any former esteem for or coveting money (L 20.27). They see their own imperfections as never before (L 20.28) and gain a new, truer humility (L 20.29). They become more detached

(L 21.6, 12). We could multiply, many times over, similar references to such effects of God's action in the soul described in both the *Life* and *The Interior Castle*.

Here again, the great teacher of prayer offers images to aid our understanding. She tells us that the effects of the prayer of union in the sixth dwellings are like the jewels that the Bridegroom gives to his beloved. In this case, she identifies those jewels as knowledge of the grandeur of God, deeper self-knowledge and humility, and little esteem for earthly things (IC 6.5.10–11). Or alternately, she says that the virtues are like flowers that bloom as the Lord passes through the garden of the soul (L 14.9) or like flowers whose fragrance is evidence of the divine work (L 17.3) and that draw others to God (L 19.3).

THE THREE VIRTUES AS GIFT

The three necessary virtues in particular—which played such an essential role in preparing for the gift of contemplation—are now, like the others, the fruit of prayer. We will look at love of neighbor in greater detail in the final section of the chapter. For Teresa, it is the crowning effect of union with God (as one would expect when God is love itself).

Detachment seems almost an inevitable effect of profound prayer and union with God. Once one has experienced true communion with the divine, how can anything that is merely a creature satisfy? She tells us that arriving at truly contemplative prayer (the "second waters" in *The Book of Her Life* or, in terms of *The Interior Castle*, the contemplative prayer of quiet), "In arriving here [the soul] begins soon to lose its craving for earthly things—and little wonder! It clearly sees that one moment of the enjoyment of glory cannot be experienced here below, neither are there riches, or sovereignties, or honors, or delights that are able to provide a brief moment of that happiness, for it is a true happiness that, it is seen, satisfies us" (L 14.5; see also L 21.12). The "vanities" of this world are revealed for what they are so that they cause no longer attraction but contempt (L 19.2; 38.18).

Once one has experienced true contemplative prayer and union, she says, "all things seemed to me like an ant-hill" (L 39.22). It seems to the person of deep prayer that "worldly delights are like filth" (IC 4.3.9). Yet more strongly, she remarks, "For the contempt that was left in me for everything earthly was great; these things all seemed to me like dung, and I see how basely we are occupied, those of us who are detained by earthly things" (L 38.3). Of course, Teresa is not devaluing the goodness of God's work of creation. She is telling us instead that, once one has truly encountered the Creator, by comparison, created things lose their attraction as something worthy of distracting, detaining, or enslaving us. "Everything wearies it [the person]," she tells us, "for it has learned through experience that creatures cannot give it true rest" (IC 5.2.8; see also L 21.6). As we have seen, for Teresa, true detachment must pass from the exterior to the interior. And the praying person at this stage becomes detached even from self-interest (see L 19.3).

But the detachment of those who have experienced union with God is not simply the logical consequence of this encounter with the Creator. God, in fact, gives a freedom from attachment that makes what was previously accomplished by graced effort seem like nothing (IC 5.2.8). In a famous passage from *The Book of Her Life*, Teresa tells us that God freed her from her attachment to certain friendships. She heard the following words: "No longer do I want you to converse with men but with angels" (L 24.5). In that instant, Teresa found herself free: "May God be blessed forever because in an instant He gave me the freedom that I with all the efforts of many years could not attain

by myself" (L 24.8). In fact, she found that she had become inca-
pable of forming any friendship based on superficial attachment
or finding consolation in an imperfect love (see L 24.6).

In the same way, contemplative prayer and union produce
a more authentic humility as a fruit. Those who are so blessed
recognize that they do not deserve what they have experienced,
nor have they in any way made it happen: "Its humility is deeper
because it sees plainly that through no diligence of its own did
it receive that very generous and magnificent gift and that it
played no role in obtaining or experiencing it" (L 19.2). Such
divine gifts do not make us proud but rather increase our humility. If people think they have experienced some supernatural
prayer but do not find themselves less concerned for honors or
less quick to take offense, they would have every reason to doubt
that their experience was an authentic one (see W 36.8).

Just as other created things lose their luster in comparison
with God, so too the person comes to see the self in a similar way (L 28.9). In light of more profound encounters with
God, one now comes to a deeper awareness of past sins, seen
now more profoundly as ingratitude. There is no fear of hell
or punishment—one has truly encountered the God who is
mercy—but the praying person is more firmly resolved to avoid
anything that might "offend" God who has been so good (IC
6.7.1–4; 7.3.14). Namely, God gives a deeper self-knowledge
that, as we saw much earlier, means holding together a vision of
God, of ourselves as the image of God, and the reality and possibility of our sin (L 15.14).

In sum, God gives the person a more genuine self-dominion—
the liberated freedom to give oneself to God—that was the goal
of the essential virtues (L 38.4). Our work of growing in these
virtues leads to the freedom to embrace and to respond to God's
self-offer. God deepens that freedom so that our self-giving can

reach the total surrender that is the transforming union of spiritual marriage.

WE STILL NEED VIGILANCE

Despite the deepening transformation that is accomplished by God, we must continue to do what is in our power to grow in virtue and avoid occasions of sin (IC 4.3.10; 5.4.5; W 31.11). There can still remain subtle inclinations to sin that Teresa calls little worms that can gnaw away at the virtues (such as self-love, an overestimation of self, a tendency to judge others, and a lack of charity toward others). None of these, at this stage, reach the status of sin, but they are traces of our inclination to sin (IC 5.3.6). Even having attained the prayer of union in the fifth dwelling places, "we should walk with special care and attention, observing how we are proceeding in the practice of virtue . . . especially in love for one another, in the desire to be considered least . . . and in the performance of ordinary tasks" (IC 5.4.9).

Teresa tells us that, even in the seventh dwelling places, the person remains capable of imperfections and even venial sin, though never intentionally. Union with God is not truly complete until one passes into the next life. And so, even a person of such profound prayer must remain vigilant and continue to call on God for help (IC 7.4.3).

SUFFERING AND TRANSFORMATION

The experience of union with God brings with it a deepening transformation of the person. But in the sixth dwelling places where union has become frequent and consistent enough to be called "spiritual betrothal," God brings about a still deeper transformation through suffering. These are, Teresa tells us, the "interior and exterior trials the soul suffers before entering the seventh dwelling place!" (IC 6.1.1).

The trials that Teresa describes are many and varied. As extraordinary experiences become known, the person suffers from gossip, ridicule, misunderstanding, and even broken friendships (IC 6.1.3). As Teresa describes in her own early struggles, the person may encounter confessors and other spiritual advisors who are inexperienced, unlearned, or fearful and who can misunderstand and offer bad advice (IC 6.1.8–9). Praise for one's perceived holiness brings even greater suffering than criticism and doubt, since the person feels his or her own unworthiness (IC 6.1.4–5). This suffering manifests itself in illnesses and great pain, exterior and interior (IC 6.1.6–7).

Ever deeper experiences of union with God have filled the person with a deepest possible longing for God. At the same time, it is ever more evident that an infinite distance remains between the self and God. The person feels caught—"left hanging"—between earth and heaven (see IC 6.11.5). Teresa compares this suffering with purgatory, and like it, it is meant to purify the person for full union with God (IC 6.11.6). By these means, "our great God wants us to know our own misery and that He is king; and this is very important for what lies ahead" (IC 6.1.12). These trials, in the end, enable the soul to "fly higher" (IC 6.2.1).

Teresa also describes the same experience in the twentieth chapter of *The Book of Her Life*. The person is overcome by pain, desolation and weariness. "God places it in a desert so distant from all things that, however much it labors, it doesn't find a creature on earth that might accompany it—nor would it want to find one; it desires only to die in that solitude" (L 20.9). There is intense pain and an extreme sense of solitude linked with the deepest yearning for God (L 20.10). "It seems to me that the soul is crucified since no consolation comes to it from heaven, nor is it in heaven; neither does it desire any from earth, nor is it on earth. Receiving no help from either side, it is as though crucified between heaven and earth" (L 20.11). And yet, the suffering is accompanied paradoxically by a great happiness: "It is an arduous, delightful martyrdom" (L 20.11). Experiencing this suffering at the time she was writing her *Life*, Teresa says, "I am oblivious of everything in that anxious longing to see God; that desert and solitude seem to the soul better than all the companionship of the world" (L 20.13). Again, the experience is like purgatory. "In this pain the soul is purified and fashioned or purged like gold in the crucible" (L 20.16).

Kieran Kavanaugh suggests that this experience can be seen as akin to the purifying reality of the "dark night" described by St. John of the Cross. He summarizes Teresa's description: "In its relationships with others, the soul experiences total incomprehension and isolation. In its psychological dynamism, an interior darkness and powerlessness comes over the soul. In its relationship with God, it experiences feelings of his absence and being abandoned by him."[1] Like the dark night of John of the Cross, this experience of suffering in the sixth dwellings brings about the transformation that prepares the person for the transforming union.

TRANSFORMED BY LOVE AND FOR LOVE

The experience of union in the fifth dwelling places brings a sleep or a suspension of consciousness ("of the faculties"). This may become more dramatic—at least for some people—in the sixth dwellings in which the person can experience ecstasies, raptures, and flights of the spirit. Teresa describes such experiences

---

1. Kieran Kavanaugh and Carol Lisi, *The Interior Castle*, study ed. (Washington, D.C.: ICS Publications, 2010), 231.

as the feeling of being taken outside one's self. But this experience changes in the seventh dwelling places in which the union
with God becomes constant and stable. In the seventh dwelling
places, one has passed beyond occasional, if profound, experiences of union and has entered into an abiding union for which
Teresa uses the image of the "one flesh" union of man and woman
in marriage. No longer pulled out of itself and abiding now in a
true union with God, the person wills what God wills and loves
as God loves. In this sense, it is only "natural" that the person in
divine union will love others as God does.

Already in the fifth dwellings, Teresa had made clear that
authentic prayer and union must lead to greater practical love
of neighbor. If a sister is at prayer, she says, experiencing spiritual delight and devotion, she should not be reluctant to leave
it behind to respond to another's genuine need. Our principal
concern must not be prayer experiences, regardless of their
type or depth: "No, Sisters, absolutely not; works are what the
Lord wants! He desires that if you see a Sister who is sick to
whom you can bring some relief, you have compassion on her
and not worry about losing this devotion" (IC 5.3.11). "I have
said a lot on this subject elsewhere, because I see, Sisters, that
if we fail in love of neighbor we are lost" (IC 5.3.12).[2] If we
see ourselves lacking in this willingness to show love in practical ways, we have serious reason to doubt the authenticity of
our prayer and union, no matter how profound the experience
may seem. Authentic union with God must yield deeper love
of neighbor in action.

---

2. Kavanaugh indicates that she is referring to her discussion of the love of neighbor in chapter 7 of *The Way of Perfection* and chapter 5 of *The Book of Foundations* (ibid., 194n229). In the
latter, she tells us that trying to remain in prayer when others are in need of our immediate attention would be like wanting to continue to gaze at Christ for our own sake while he is asking us to
do what is more pleasing to him (see F 5.5).

Teresa tells us in chapter 3 of the seventh dwellings that the spiritual marriage with God yields abundant fruit in our lives: forgetfulness of self, the desire to suffer, deep interior joy in persecution, the desire to serve, great detachment, and an absence of fear of the devil's deceits.[3] In the fourth and final chapter of *The Interior Castle*, she tells us that it is love that has been the purpose of all that has gone before. It would be a "serious error" to think that the mystical gifts have been given for the spiritual delight of the one receiving them (IC 7.4.4). "This is the reason for prayer, my daughters, the purpose of this spiritual marriage: the birth always of good works, good works" (IC 7.4.6). Such love is a true sign of authentic favors from God, of whatever kind (IC 7.4.7). She challenges her readers: "Let us desire and be occupied in prayer not for the sake of our enjoyment but so as to have strength to serve" (IC 7.4.12).

One might imagine that once we have arrived at the innermost chamber of the interior castle and entered into abiding union with God, we would now be totally absorbed in God and oblivious to the surrounding world, leaving the needs of others to more "active" persons. But this is not the case at all, nor is it the witness that Teresa gave in her own life. Even after she had reached the heights of prayer, she remained decidedly active and involved in the growth of the Carmelite reform and concerned for the needs of the church and the world's peoples, or "souls" everywhere.[4]

---

3. Ibid., 416n396.

4. Teresa received abiding union with God or the "spiritual marriage" in 1572 (see ST 31). She lived another ten very active years, during which her attention was frequently turned beyond the Carmelite reform. Her extant letters from this period, especially, reveal her attentive wider concern for evangelization in the New World, the advance of the Reformation, the spiritual and physical good of her immediate family, as well as uprisings, epidemics, and wars. Union with God most definitely did not result in an inward turn or isolation for St. Teresa. See Tomás Alvarez, *St. Teresa of Avila: 100 Themes on Her Life and Work*, trans. Kieran Kavanaugh (Washington, DC: ICS Publications, 2011), 397.

In a wonderful interpretation of the well-known Gospel story of Martha and Mary welcoming Jesus into their home (Lk 10:38–42), Teresa says that the two come to work together to show true hospitality to the Lord (IC 7.4.12–14; W 31.5; M 7.3). Traditionally, Martha, busy with details of hospitality, has been interpreted to represent the active life of service of others. Mary, on the other hand, who sat quietly listening at the feet of Jesus, represents the contemplative life. But here, at the very end of *The Interior Castle*'s description of the journey into divine union, Teresa masterfully brings the two together—not one or the other, not one over the other, but Martha and Mary working together as different sides of offering hospitality to Christ. The person in abiding union with God cannot but reach out to others.

The love to which we are compelled is not something idealized or even usually expressed in extraordinary actions (IC 7.4.14). It is a love manifest in ordinary deeds of service for the flesh-and-blood people we find before us each day. "In sum, my Sisters, what I conclude is that we shouldn't build castles in the air. The Lord doesn't look so much at the greatness of our works as at the love with which they are done. . . . Thus even if our works are small, they will have the value our love for him would have merited had they been great" (IC 7.4.15).

The fact that the way of transformation reaches its culmination in this life with the challenge to love demonstrates that Teresa's vision of the human person and of the spiritual path is neither individualistic nor exclusively inward looking. We have seen throughout our reflection on this journey that Teresa has urged—even as her own life in all its phases demonstrates—practical love for others. The freedom that this journey has sought and promoted is precisely the liberty to love God and neighbor fully and freely. Now, in describing the seventh dwellings and the deepest union with God possible in this life, Teresa reveals even more fully her relational, communal, and ecclesial vision—a vision rooted in her own experience of God.

LOVE IS OUR IDENTITY

Teresa saw with abundant clarity the beauty of the human person created in the image of God. She knew from the depth of her own mystical experience that we are made for union with God—a God who dwells within each of us, at the very center of our being. The God who dwells within each of us is love, calling us to love God and neighbor. In this God who dwells within us, we encounter the divine love for everyone else. For Teresa, as one noted commentator puts it, "God is the place of encounter with other people."[5] Having entered into the deepest union possible in this life with the God who is love, how could we not confront the challenge to reach out to others with a still greater and more effective loving in practice?

> The freedom that this journey has sought and promoted is precisely the liberty to love God and neighbor fully and freely.

To say it another way, we are created in the image of a God who is love. Love is not just an attitude, attribute, or activity of God. God *is* love. At the heart of the triune God in whose image we are made is the eternal mutual love of the Three Persons. Since we are created in the image of God (*imago dei*), we are

---

5. Maximiliano Herráiz, *Solo Dios Basta: Claves de la espiritualidad teresiana*, 5th ed. (Madrid: Editorial de Espiritualidad, 2000), 284.

also created in the image of the Trinity (*imago trinitatis*). And so, being the divine image, we are made to love. Love is what we were made to do and to be. Love of God and neighbor is what we are made for. Doing it perfectly, Teresa says, would be our perfection, our fulfillment. And to the degree that we do not yet fully love God and neighbor, we are neither truly ourselves nor truly in union with God.[6] In the end, the way of transformation makes us who we truly are—in God.

---

6. Ibid., 288.

CONCLUSION

—⚜—

THE SILKWORM, THE COCOON, AND THE BUTTERFLY

I n the second chapter of the fifth dwelling places, Teresa introduces a key image for the work of transformation: the silkworm, the cocoon, and the butterfly. She herself tells us that the image "is good for making us see how, even though we can do nothing in this work done by our Lord [bringing us into union], we can do much by disposing ourselves so that His Majesty can grant us this favor" (IC 5.2.1). A closer look at Teresa's unfolding of this metaphor will provide a good summary of her way of transformation.

The silkworm, which is fat and ugly, she tells us, nourishes itself on mulberry leaves. When it is fully grown, it begins to spin the cocoon of silk in which it will enclose itself. It dies within the cocoon but emerges transformed as a pretty white butterfly.[1] We are like this silkworm. The Holy Spirit gives us life, and we begin to nourish ourselves on the common spiritual food given to us by God and the church: reconciliation and the other sacraments, good books, taking good homilies to heart and studying

---

1. Teresa doesn't have the biology of it quite right: she thinks that the silkworm comes from seeds brought to life in warm weather and that it actually dies in its cocoon to be reborn. Instead, we now know, the silkworm itself undergoes a process of true metamorphosis. Also, she uses the terms "butterfly" and "moth" interchangeably. See Kieran Kavanaugh and Carol Lisi, *The Interior Castle*, study ed. (Washington, D.C.: ICS Publications, 2010), 188n218.

our Catholic faith, and meditation. Teresa indicates that she has been describing this process of growth in the first four dwelling places.[2] All of this is our effort at preparing ourselves to receive the divine gift of contemplation and union.

But when we reach spiritual maturity, we begin to spin the cocoon that she tells us is really Christ. We begin to weave this cocoon which is Christ by ridding ourselves of "self-love and self-will, our attachments to any earthly thing, and by performing deeds of penance, prayer, mortification, obedience, and of all the other things you know" (IC 5.2.6). In truth, it is God who joins our labors to the divine action in Christ so that, quoting St. Paul, "our life is hidden in Christ" (IC 5.2.4; see Col 3:3–4). Teresa herself admits that the parallel struggles a bit at this point, since we cannot, on our own, put ourselves in or "build up" Christ like a cocoon. But she intends for us to see that we must reach the point at which God takes over, and we enter into Christ's own dying and rising.

When God draws the soul into union in these fifth dwellings, the soul is like the silkworm, dead in its cocoon. It emerges transformed, just as the silkworm dies and is transformed into the butterfly. "How transformed the soul is when it comes out of this prayer after having been placed within the greatness of God and so closely joined with him for a little while—in my opinion the union never lasts for as much as a half hour" (IC 5.2.7). Although the experience of union is brief and will deepen in the following dwellings, union with God (not just encounter or presence) transforms us in God. The transformation has now become entirely God's work, with our continuing cooperation and commitment. Later in this same chapter, Teresa will use the image of a seal pressed into hot wax to leave its imprint as an

---

2. Ibid., 174n207.

image of our passivity or receptivity to God's action in our transformation (IC 5.2.12).

The resulting transformation is amazing even to the person: "Truly, I tell you that the soul doesn't recognize itself. Look at the difference there is between an ugly worm and a little white butterfly; that's what the difference is here" (IC 5.2.7). As always, Teresa moves immediately to the effects or fruits of this experience of union and its transformation: the person has an overpowering desire to praise God, together with an eagerness for trials, for penance, for solitude, that all might know God and refrain from offending God (IC 5.2.7). Having experienced union with God, the person is now totally dissatisfied with what the world has to offer and becomes yet more free of excessive attachment to persons or created things (IC 5.2.8).

There is yet more that God must do in the sixth and seventh dwellings, and individuals at this stage must remain vigilant and not allow themselves to fall back. But the experience of the transformation that remains is fundamentally different. People look back on their previous labors at weaving the cocoon but see now that they have the power from God to soar like a butterfly (IC 5.2.8).

The death of the silkworm is a metaphor for the paschal mystery. We must die with Christ in order that God may bring us to newness of life. This is the heart of the Christian life, and indeed every authentic human life: "Let it die; let this silkworm die, as it does completing what it was created to do" (IC 5.2.6). But more than "let" it die, Teresa tells us that we ourselves must do what we can to put the silkworm to death (IC 5.3.5). In all of this, Teresa is speaking of a powerful experience of the paschal mystery—dying and rising to new life—which is a profound deepening of our union with Christ in baptism as well as a true anticipation of the final and eternal union of heaven.

Passing from the second chapter of the fifth dwellings to the third chapter, Teresa further unfolds the image of the silkworm by telling us that the little butterfly must give forth the seed that will produce other silkworms; that is, God wants the divine favor to bear fruit for the benefit of others (IC 5.3.1). For Teresa, authentic union with God always moves us to focus on love for others. And so, this third chapter is devoted to love of neighbor.

Here (IC 5.3.5), Teresa makes a distinction between the "delightful union" that is the infused union of prayer and another union that is the conformity of our wills with God.[3] For her, the latter is the more fundamental: "This union with God's will is the union I have desired all my life; it is the union I ask the Lord for always and the one that is clearest and safest" (IC 5.3.5). And conformity to the divine will necessarily means, at heart, union with the divine loving: "The Lord asks of us only two things: love of His Majesty and love of our neighbor. These are what we must work for. By observing them with perfection, we do His will and so will be united with Him" (IC 5.3.7). The "delightful" union of infused prayer both presupposes this correspondence with the divine will and serves its more complete and more rapid attainment.

Teresa picks up the image of the butterfly again in the final dwellings. In the fifth dwellings, she had described the death of the silkworm and its transformation into a butterfly. But here in the seventh dwellings she tells us that the little butterfly itself dies because in the transforming union of spiritual marriage, it dies with joy because its life is now Christ (IC 7.2.5; see also Phil 1:21). Again, as always, she immediately describes the effects of this new life. Kavanaugh summarizes them in this way:

---

3. Ibid., 190n224, 190n225. The distinction is apparent in the title of the third chapter: "Tells about another kind of union the soul can reach with God's help and of how important love of neighbor is for this union."

forgetfulness of self, the desire to suffer, deep interior joy in persecution, the desire to serve, great detachment, and no fear of the devil's deceits.[4] It is easy to see that these effects are largely the essential virtues but now more perfectly realized, not as a result of our graced efforts but as the fruit of union with God.

Embracing the Way of Transformation

The way of "perfection" laid out by St. Teresa is a way of transformation. Through our own graced efforts and increasingly through the work of God in deepening prayer, we are ultimately transformed through union with God in Christ. The way of transformation is not only a matter of prayer, but also effectively of life remade, reborn in Christ.

Teresa is an unsurpassed teacher of prayer, and we rightly turn to her to learn the ways of prayer. But hope for growth in the prayer and union that she describes can come about only by taking up the hard work of preparation that she teaches so insistently. Although it is true that the real work of conversion is truly and ultimately God's, the fruits of life-changing union can come only to those who have diligently made themselves fruitful ground for it. It is our growing conformity to God's

> The way of transformation is not only a matter of prayer, but also effectively of life remade, reborn in Christ.

---

4. Ibid., 416n396. Kavanaugh explains that he provides the summary because Teresa unfolds the effects in the midst of digressions.

loving—to the degree that it is in our capacity to do so—that creates the conditions in which the gift of divine union can be received. We will finally and truly embrace the inflow of the divine self-giving love and respond completely when we have reached the point of liberating our freedom to give ourselves in return.

Certainly, the particular tools that Teresa offers—the three essential virtues of love of neighbor, detachment, and humility, pursued with a determined determination—can be understood in different ways with differing emphases. Every "school" of Christian spirituality has offered its own version and its own particular accents. But the key point is that every school of spirituality in the long Christian tradition has in fact insisted on the kind of preparation that Teresa lays out so classically and with such particular insight. Few, if any, have intertwined our human efforts at transformation so closely with powerful descriptions and insightful teachings on prayer.

St. Teresa has offered us unsurpassed teaching for attaining the truly unimaginable wonder of union with and transformation in God. Let's study faithfully and embrace wholeheartedly the path as she lays it out for us so that we may all arrive at our truest fulfillment in abiding union with our God.

Questions for Reflection/Discussion

Introduction

1. In what ways do you think that your life might need to be transformed? What does a "new and better" you look like in the actual circumstances of your life?

2. Have you thought about how your daily living impacts your prayer or about how your prayer bears fruit in your ordinary living? Why is it important to see this connection?

3. What do you think you might have to change about your attitudes or ways of acting in order to be more fertile ground for prayer?

One: The Path of Transformation: The Big Picture

1. Do you find Teresa's image of the soul as an interior castle with concentric layers of dwelling places helpful? There's a saying that "every comparison limps." Is there anything in this image of the soul and of the spiritual journey that seems to you to be missing or incomplete?

2. What are the "poisonous creatures" from outside your own personal interior castle that are trying to pull you back out of the interior journey? How do you resist them or deal with them?

3. Do you think you understand what Teresa is saying about the experience of the more interior dwelling places? Are they appealing to you? Does anything in her description concern you or seem off-putting?

4. The idea that the Christian journey is an inner pathway to God who dwells within us might seem to be individualistic, isolated, or too interior. How does Teresa's teaching prevent her readers from going in that direction? Does she seem successful?

Two: The Journey Begins

1. In what way do you think human persons are the image of God? How can we better mirror the reality of God or serve as God's true images in our daily lives?

2. What does the reality of sin mean to you? How is it manifest in your life? Have you ever thought about how sin might mar or disguise the image of God in you?

3. Teresa urges us to overcome, as much as we can, even our venial sins. That seems like a tall order! What are the venial sins upon which you should focus at this point in your spiritual journey?

4. What is Teresa talking about when she says that many people "live outside their own castle"? Would that phrase describe you in any way, at any point in your life?

5. What does Teresa mean when she urges us to self-knowledge? Why is it so important to her?

Three: Prayer and the Three Necessary Virtues

1. Were you familiar with Teresa's distinctions between vocal prayer, mental prayer, meditation, and contemplation? Do they make sense to you? With these distinctions in mind, how can you deepen your own prayer?

2. Have you ever tried a technique to become recollected in prayer? In what did the technique consist? Was it helpful? Have you felt that God suddenly calmed and focused you in prayer?

3. Why does Teresa insist so much on the development of these three necessary virtues? What is so essential about them in relation to growth in prayer?

4. In what way is growth in freedom—the liberation of our freedom—necessary to growth in prayer?

5. God wants to give the divine life to each one of us—to fill us with the divine presence. What stands in the way of your free self-gift to God?

FOUR: Love for Others

1. How would you define for others the most basic meaning of love? What is a one-sentence definition of the love to which Christ calls us?

2. If love is our identity, why is it sometimes so hard? What— in you—makes it difficult for you to love others? How could you more effectively show your love for others in practical, daily ways?

3. Where, in your own life, have you seen the clearest examples of love? What, for you, characterizes a truly loving person? How have you experienced being loved?

4. What does Teresa mean when she speaks of the two kinds of love? She says she had trouble explaining the distinction. How would you explain it to others?

5. Have you ever experienced an unhealthy love when your love for someone—or his or her love for you—was too needy or attached? How does your love for your family and friends—and their love for you—draw you closer to God or hold you back?

6. Are there limits to loving or to self-giving? What are they? Have you ever been in a particular situation or relationship in which it seemed to you that self-forgetfulness was the wrong response? Why?

FIVE: DETACHMENT

1. Do you think you are "attached" to superficial things? Do you possess anything that in fact might really possess you? If so, what? Does it hinder you or control your life and decisions in any way?

2. We live in a materialistic and consumerist culture. How do you think it impacts you? How might you contribute to it?

3. Have you ever found it helpful to your spiritual life or discipline to deny yourself something? Have you ever found fasting helpful to your spiritual growth? Why or why not?

4. Do you take care of your health? Do you think you might be overly concerned about your body, your health, natural aging, or the reality of death? Have you ever experienced a tension between caring for your health and some spiritual practice that seemed worthwhile to you?

5. Teresa encourages us to think of the ways that God has already made us rich. In what ways are you already blessed by God? How do you imagine or think about the blessings that God wants to give you?

SIX: HUMILITY: TO WALK IN TRUTH

1. Does humility really seem like an important virtue to you in your spiritual life? Do you think you are a humble person? Why or why not?

2. For Teresa, humility consists in the recognition of God's greatness and mercy as well as our status as creatures and sinners. Do you think you reflect enough, or too much, on your sin? Does that seem helpful to you? Do you practice the traditional recommendation of a daily examination of conscience? If so, what do you typically see in your daily self-reviews?

3. Have you ever given up the practice of prayer because you felt unworthy or too sinful? Has the feeling of unworthiness or the awareness of sin held you back from some spiritual or vocational goal? What would Teresa recommend?

4. Are you someone who takes offense easily? Are you easily hurt by others? Have you ever thought that you might describe yourself as "petty" when it comes to your reaction to people and situations?

5. In our day and age, we don't have the same concern for "honor" that Teresa criticized in her culture. But do you find in yourself concern for status, "keeping up with" or "getting ahead of" others, or being well thought of by others?

6. Have you ever given up prayer because it didn't "feel good"? How important is it to your practice of and fidelity to prayer that you experience what Teresa calls "consolations" in prayer?

SEVEN: *Muy Determinada Determinación:* A very determined determination

1. Are you a determined person? Do you feel you are someone who sticks to a project or the effort to attain a goal, or do you tend to give up after a while? Can you think of examples?

2. Are you a patient person? Growth in prayer usually requires us to be engaged "for the long haul." Do you find you are persevering and patient enough on the way?

3. Do you make New Year's resolutions? What's been your record of keeping them? If you have failed to keep them, when you look back, do you think you had really been determined from the very beginning?

4. Do you have a "very determined determination" when it comes to prayer? Are you faithful to your prayer even when it feels dry?

5. Teresa uses military or battle images to teach about determination and fortitude. Can you think of other ways you might explain or encourage determination in people of today?

6. Do you have "lofty" or "noble" goals when it comes to your spiritual life? Why or why not? Is holiness, contemplative prayer, or union with God in this life a real goal for you, or have you set your sights lower? Have you set out with determination? If not, why not?

EIGHT: Transformed by Prayer

1. Have you ever noticed in your life that faithful prayer yields good fruit in your attitudes and ways of living and relating to others?

2. How have you been transformed by suffering in your own life? How are you better or perhaps worse for the ways you have reacted to difficulties in your life?

3. What do you think of Teresa's interpretation of the Gospel story of Martha and Mary? How would you explain it to others?

CONCLUSION: The Silkworm, the Cocoon, and the Butterfly

1. Does Teresa's use of the image of the silkworm and butterfly seem helpful to you? Why or why not? Can you think of other images for transformation?

2. St. Paul tells us that "our life is hidden in Christ." How does Teresa understand the meaning of that text? Does it seem to have any meaning in your life? If so, how?

3. In what way, for Teresa, is the "way of perfection" also a "way of transformation"?

Select Bibliography

STUDY EDITIONS OF ST. TERESA'S WORKS

The Book of Her Foundations. Study Guide. Prepared by Marc Foley. Translated by Kieran Kavanaugh and Otilio Rodriguez. Washington, D.C.: ICS Publications, 2011.

The Interior Castle. Study Edition. Prepared by Kieran Kavanaugh and Carol Lisi. Translated by Kieran Kavanaugh and Otilio Rodriguez. Washington, D.C.: ICS Publications, 2010.

The Way of Perfection. Study Edition. Prepared by Kieran Kavanaugh. Translated by Kieran Kavanaugh and Otilio Rodriguez. Washington, D.C.: ICS Publications, 2000.

COLLECTED WORKS

The Collected Letters of St. Teresa of Avila. Translated by Kieran Kavanaugh. 2 vols. Washington, D.C.: ICS Publications, 2001–2007.

The Collected Works of St. Teresa of Avila. Translated by Kieran Kavanaugh and Otilio Rodriguez. Rev. ed. 3 vols. Washington, D.C.: ICS Publications, 1985–2012.

The Complete Works of St. Teresa. Translated by E. Allison Peers. 3 vols. London: Sheed and Ward, 1946.

St. Teresa of Avila and St. John of the Cross: The Collected Works and Letters. Carmelite Digital Library. CD-ROM, version 2.0. Washington, D.C.: Carmelite Clarion Communications, 2003–2011.

This CD-ROM includes the Spanish texts of Teresa and John's works, as well as the Kavanaugh-Rodriguez and the Peers translations; the Douay-Rheims translation of the Bible; and search tools.

Secondary Sources in English

Ahlgren, Gillian T. *Entering Teresa of Avila's Interior Castle: A Reader's Companion*. Mahwah, N.J.: Paulist Press, 2005.

Álvarez, Tomás. *St. Teresa of Avila: 100 Themes on Her Life and Work*. Translated by Kieran Kavanaugh. Washington, D.C.: ICS Publications, 2011.

Álvarez, Tomás, and Fernando Domingo. *The Divine Adventure: St. Teresa of Avila's Journeys and Foundations*. Translated by Christopher O'Mahony and Patricia Lynn Morrison. Washington, D.C.: ICS Publications, 2015.

Bilinkoff, Jodi. *The Avila of Saint Teresa: Religious Reform in a Sixteenth Century City*. Ithaca, N.Y.: Cornell University Press, 1989.

Luti, J. Mary. *Teresa of Avila's Way*. Way of the Christian Mystics 13. Edited by Noel Dermot O'Donoghue. Collegeville, Minn.: Liturgical Press, 1991.

Mujica, Bárbara. *Teresa of Avila: Lettered Woman*. Nashville: Vanderbilt University Press, 2009.

Seelaus, Vilma. *Distractions in Prayer: Blessing or Curse? St. Teresa of Avila's Teaching in The Interior Castle*. Staten Island, N.Y.: St. Paul's Publications, 2005.

Simsic, Wayne. *The Inward Path to God: A Prayer Journey with St. Teresa of Avila*. Frederick, Md.: Word Among Us Press, 2015.

Williams, Rowan. *Teresa of Avila*. New York: Continuum, 1991.

Secondary Works in Spanish

Álvarez, Tomás. *Comentarios a las obras de Santa Teresa de Jesús: Libro de la Vida, Camino de Perfección, Castillo Interior*. Burgos, Spain: Editorial Monte Carmelo, 2005.

———. ed. *Diccionario de Santa Teresa: Doctrina e Historia*. 2nd ed. Burgos, Spain: Editorial Monte Carmelo, 2006.

Barrientos, Alberto, ed. *Introducción a la lectura de Santa Teresa*. 2nd ed. Madrid: Editorial de Espiritualidad, 2002.

Castro, Secundino. *Ser cristiano según Santa Teresa: Teología y espiritualidad*. 2nd ed. Madrid: Editorial de Espiritualidad, 1985.

Egido, Teófanes, et al. *Perfil histórico de Santa Teresa*. 3rd ed. Madrid: Editorial de Espiritualidad, 1981.

Herráiz Garcia, Maximilano. *Introducción al Camino de Perfección de Teresa de Jesús*. Burgos, Spain: Editorial Monte Carmelo, 2001.

———. *Introducción al Castillo Interior de Teresa de Jesús*. Burgos, Spain: Editorial Monte Carmelo, 2001.

———. *Introducción al Libro de la Vida de Teresa de Jesús*. Burgos, Spain: Editorial Monte Carmelo, 2001.

———. *Solo Dios Basta: Claves de la espiritualidad teresiana*. 5th ed. Madrid: Editorial de Espiritualidad, 2000.

———. *A Zaga de tu huella: Escritos teresiano-sanjuanistas y de espiritualidad*. Burgos, Spain: Editorial Monte Carmelo, 2004.

Maroto, Daniel de Pablo. *Teresa en oración: Historia, Experiencia, Doctrina*. Madrid: Editorial de Espiritualidad, 2004.

Sancho, Francisco-Javier Fermín, and Romulo Londoño Cuartas, eds. *Camino de Perfección de Santa Teresa de Jesús*. Actas del II Congreso Internacional Teresiano en preparación del V Centenario de su nacimiento (1515–2015). Burgos, Spain: Editorial Monte Carmelo, 2012.

———. eds. *Vivir en Ávila cuando Santa Teresa escribió el Libro de su Vida*. Ávila, Spain: CITeS, 2011.

OTHER MEDIA

Egan, Keith J. *Exploring the Interior Castle: The Mystical Wisdom of St. Teresa of Avila*. Rockville, Md.: Now You Know Media, 2014. Audio CD collection of twelve lectures with study guide.

———. *Teresa, Teach Us to Pray*. Rockville, Md.: Now You Know Media, 2011. Audio CD collection of twelve lectures with study guide.

See also various lectures by Carmelite authors on audio CD sets available from Carmelite Clarion Communications, Washington, D.C. Full listing available at *http://www.CarmelClarion.com*.

Other Books by Mark O'Keefe, O.S.B.

Love Awakened by Love: The Liberating Ascent of Saint John of the Cross
ICS Publications, 2014

Deciding to Be Christian: A Daily Commitment
Liguori, 2012

Priestly Wisdom: Insights from St. Benedict
Abbey Press, 2004

Priestly Prayer: Reflections on Prayer in the Life of the Priest
Abbey Press, 2002

Priestly Virtues: Reflections on the Moral Virtues in the Life of the Priest
Abbey Press, 2000

The Ordination of a Priest: Reflections on the Priesthood in the Rite of Ordination
Abbey Press, 1999

In Persona Christi: Reflections on Priestly Identity and Holiness
Abbey Press, 1998

Becoming Good, Becoming Holy: On the Relationship of Christian Ethics and Spirituality
Paulist Press, 1995; St. Pauls/India, 1997; St. Pauls/Philippines, 1997

What Are They Saying About Social Sin?
Paulist Press, 1990

Index

About Us

ICS Publications, based in Washington, D.C., is the publishing house of the Institute of Carmelite Studies (ICS) and a ministry of the Discalced Carmelite Friars of the Washington Province (U.S.A.). The Institute of Carmelite Studies promotes research and publication in the field of Carmelite spirituality, especially about Carmelite saints and related topics. Its members are friars of the Washington Province.

Discalced Carmelites are a worldwide Roman Catholic religious order comprised of friars, nuns, and laity—men and women who are heirs to the teaching and way of life of Teresa of Avila and John of the Cross, dedicated to contemplation and to ministry in the church and the world.

Information about their way of life is available through local diocesan vocation offices, or from the Discalced Carmelite Friars vocation directors at the following addresses:

Washington Province:
1525 Carmel Road, Hubertus, WI 53033

California-Arizona Province:
P.O. Box 3420, San Jose, CA 95156

Oklahoma Province:
5151 Marylake Drive, Little Rock, AR 72206

Visit our websites at:

www.icspublications.org and *http://ocdfriarsvocation.org*